Authentic
SPANISH
COOKING

Authentic
SPANISH
COOKING

Julie Neville

WHITE OWL

AN IMPRINT OF PEN & SWORD BOOKS LTD.
YORKSHIRE – PHILADELPHIA

First published in Great Britain in 2020 by
PEN & SWORD WHITE OWL
An imprint of Pen & Sword Books Ltd
Yorkshire – Philadelphia

ISBN 9781526752598

Graphic design by Paul Wilkinson.
Photography by Margarita Ferrer Mari

Printed and bound in India, by Replika Press Pvt. Ltd.

Pen & Sword Books Ltd incorporates the Imprints of Pen & Sword Books
Archaeology, Atlas, Aviation, Battleground, Discovery, Family History, History,
Maritime, Military, Naval, Politics, Railways, Select, Transport, True Crime,
Fiction, Frontline Books, Leo Cooper, Praetorian Press, Seaforth Publishing,
Wharncliffe and White Owl.

For a complete list of Pen & Sword titles please contact:

PEN & SWORD BOOKS LTD
47 Church Street, Barnsley, South Yorkshire, S70 2AS, England
E-mail: enquiries@pen-and-sword.co.uk
Website: www.pen-and-sword.co.uk

or

PEN AND SWORD BOOKS
1950 Lawrence Rd, Havertown, PA 19083, USA
E-mail: Uspen-and-sword@casematepublishers.com
Website: www.penandswordbooks.com

CONTENTS

Introduction 7

RESTAURANTE JOAQUIN SCHMIDT 11

CASA MANOLO 22

HELADOS LLINARES 34

ASKUA 42

CA PEPICO 50

KAYMUS 58

MARINA BEACH CLUB 66

LA LOLA 76

TASTAVI 86

RAUSELL 94

ASADA AURORA 112

CASA GRANERO 122

ALQUERIA DEL POU 130

CIVERA 140

RESTAURANTE GABRINUS 150

OSCAR TORRIJOS 160

CASA MONTAÑA 181

PETIT BISTRO 194

FOOD AND FUN 204

FEDERAL CAFÉ 224

COCKTAILS – Ivan & Hector Talens 236

NAVARRO BODEGUERO 244

INTRODUCTION

Ever since I was a child, I have had a real passion for cooking. I think I was one of the few students who bounded into Home Economics classes with enthusiasm. The night before each class I took great pride weighing and measuring all my ingredients precisely and placing them neatly into my cookery basket.

From a very early age, I could not wait for a Sunday morning to surprise my parents in bed with an array of freshly baked breakfast goods, from pancakes, to a full cooked breakfast, to eggs in various forms. Unfortunately for my parents, this usually occurred after a big Saturday night out and at seven in the morning when the last thing they wanted was a plate of food being dropped on their laps in bed!

As I hit my teens, I realised that, for me, not only was cooking a hobby from which I drew great enjoyment but I also found it to be extremely therapeutic and relaxing, not to mention rewarding. I am sure that any cook will tell you that there is nothing more gratifying than seeing what starts as a mix of basic ingredients coming together to produce a delicious culinary delight to be enjoyed by friends, family or customers or simply oneself. I think to steer me away from the early morning breakfast deliveries, my parents entrusted me with the catering for all their dinner parties, from starters and main courses, to appetizers and handmade chocolates as well as the everyday cooking and baking for the whole family and my passion continued to grow.

My teens passed and I met my then husband-to-be who was a professional footballer so my cooking took on a different angle of fuelling an athlete, providing him with the exact amount of protein, carbohydrates and fats that he needed for optimum performance, endurance and recovery. Timing his meals and working around his match and training schedules and learning to look at food not only as something we enjoy but as a vital part of my husband's preparation for the physical strain that his job demanded became my main focus And then came our children, firstly our son Harvey, followed a little earlier than planned by our daughter Isabella and so my passion and interest was channelled towards developing delicious and healthy homemade 'baby meals'. Every two weeks my kitchen was like a food factory where I would make five or six batches of different meals and desserts, puree them all, pour into portion size pots, label them (yes, I even bought a label printer) and then place them in the freezer. Each morning I would simply take out three different meals for the day – simple!

Then, as I was suffering from several health issues following the traumatic birth of our daughter and I had failed to recover using conventional medicines, I started to educate myself on food as medicine and this was a real eye opener for me. Even though I had previously been aware that certain foods were healthy and others not so healthy, to really learn in depth about how food can not only prevent but treat and cure a wide range of conditions was incredible and played a huge role in my personal recovery. This then led me to becoming vegetarian for almost eight years, so fillet steak and chunky chips was replaced with hearty lentil stew and black bean casserole. I actually loved every single minute of being vegetarian and often would be completely vegan. It also taught me to explore other herbs and spices as well as combining plant proteins to make whole proteins. Then came the diagnosis of being allergic to gluten. I was in denial for a while and asked for the tests to be run again as I ate as many gluten containing foods as I could until the second round of tests confirmed it and my destiny was to be a gluten-free human being. So then my cooking began to explore recipes excluding the use of gluten-containing foods. It was a challenge at the beginning, as gluten is hidden in so many foods and used in so many ways but eventually, I found my groove and added another skill to my expanding cookery CV.

So my journey with food has been varied to say the least and while I never did achieve my dream of going to cookery school to train to cook at a really high level (something that I still intend to do when time permits) I have thoroughly enjoyed the journey to date. Then four years ago, with just two weeks' notice from my husband, as a family we moved to Valencia in Spain and we took on the task of learning a new culture, new language, making new friends, finding new schools and starting a whole new life away from everything that had been important to us until this point in our lives. Make no mistake, it was a challenge but we all embraced it and I can honestly say it has been a wonderful experience. What did amaze us all was that despite being relatively close in distance to the UK what a totally different culture it is in Spain. Valencia itself is a very traditional, historic Spanish city on the East coast of Spain, with very few English speakers. It can only be described as utterly beautiful from the River Turia dried out river bed that runs through the centre of the city filled with parks, botanical gardens and sports facilities, to the crystal blue sea, to the perfect white sandy beaches, to the historic buildings and then comes the food!

Until I arrived in Valencia I thought we knew how to enjoy our food in the UK, but we could definitely learn a thing or two from the Spanish. It is not possible to buy fresh fish that is packaged with a shelf life of one week – fish has to be bought fresh daily and used on the

Valencia.

same day and the same applies to meat. Processed, pre prepared, ready-made meals do not exist. The fruit pickers can be seen in the orchards picking the fruit and vegetables first thing in the morning and the same fruit and vegetables are on the supermarket and green grocer shelves in the afternoons – they may not look perfect but my goodness they taste it. There are no sandwich shops or 'food to go' stores as the Spanish NEVER eat food on the go. Between 2pm and 4pm virtually everything comes to a halt as families and friends come together to relax and enjoy lunch which tends to be the main meal of the day and make no mistake, the Spanish put a lot of love into their cooking. People go home from work, children can go home from school to return later, shops and businesses close – it is a precious ritual. Then again in the evening (in fact usually as late as 10pm) families come together to dine and I mean the whole family from the babies to the grandmothers – all four generations if not more. It was the first thing that I noticed when I arrived here in Valencia that everyday restaurants would be filled with tables full of diners of a range of generations – not just for a family Sunday lunch or a special occasion but every day. Even the finest Michelin Star restaurants welcome the whole family and I love that as our children come everywhere with us.

Even better the Spanish have what is called 'Almuerzo' which takes place around 10.30am–11am which I suppose is our equivalent of brunch during which they eat bocadillos (baguettes), pastries, donuts etc as lunch is so late around 3pm and then at around 5pm they have 'Merienda' which I suppose our nearest equivalent would be afternoon tea, again as they dine so late and here they eat once again bocadillos, fruits, pastries, tapas – small dishes.

So that is the tradition but then to the produce, the flavours, the famous dishes – it really was something that I had never experienced before. The way the Spanish use oils and seasoning, their methods of cooking and the presentation – it was a whole new world of cooking for me and not only delicious but for the most part incredibly healthy. I had cooked what I deemed to be 'Spanish' meals in the past, I had eaten in Tapas restaurants in the UK and I had dined out on holiday in the Mediterranean many times but I soon realised I had not even scratched the surface of true Spanish cooking. As always eager to learn and expand my knowledge of food and cooking, I decided to visit some of the best Spanish eateries – these ranged not only from the very best fine restaurants but to the long standing traditional family restaurants. I tested out the tapas bars and the hidden pastelerias that bake the finest pastries and have queues the whole length of the street every day and I became a huge fan of the seafood restaurants on the beach where you can tell that just hours earlier the food you are eating was in the sea in front of you. I quickly located the finest churro bakeries (a traditional Spanish donut type pastry) as well as the home made ice cream shops (heladerias). I am pretty sure that I experienced a wide range of Spanish gastronomy.

Whilst I may never be a professional chef – other than to my children and husband – I have managed to fulfil my dream by entering the kitchens of these wonderful restaurants and having the privilege of being taught by their highly talented chefs to cook some of their most popular and famous dishes. They have taught me what dishes go well together to create the perfect Spanish style dinner party with starters, main courses and desserts as well as wines to complement, the secrets to achieving the most incredible flavours, top cooking tips and how to recreate restaurant standard food in my own kitchen quickly and easily and I am thrilled to share all that I have learned in this book. Now you too can bring a little of the Mediterranean to your kitchen from the heart healthy seafood and fish dishes to the tasty sweet treats. This has been both a wonderful journey and experience for me and I hope it will be the same for you.

I have given each dish a star rating ranging from three stars (super healthy), to one star (not so healthy). There is also a treat rating which means it should be consumed in moderation.

Remember to put love into your food –
believe me, you can taste it!

RESTAURANTE JOAQUIN SCHMIDT

Carrer de la Visitacio, 7, 46009, Valencia

This restaurant was recommended to me by my photographer Marga Ferrer who has worked for many years in the world of gastronomy and she certainly knows the who's who of chefs and restaurants in Spain and Ibiza. If you didn't know about this restaurant then you certainly wouldn't just find it, as its door is hidden, slightly set back from what is a bustling, busy city street. People walk past, chatting on their phones, rushing to meetings, laden with shopping bags, completely unaware of this wonderful gem concealed behind a rather plain wooden door. To enter, you have to press a doorbell and then you are met by Joaquin Schmidt himself who not only welcomes every single guest at the door but who is also the chef and waiter – there are no other staff! The restaurant reminded me of a gangster-run jazz club of the 1920s and I could easily imagine the mafia bosses sitting at the tables with their cigars. A strong smell of myrrh fills the whole restaurant which is quite dark and pop art and other modern art hangs from every wall. Authentic records are the placemats on each table and the wall units are filled with every bottle of spirit and wine, all thick with dust which only adds to the authenticity of this extraordinary restaurant.

And then the food … which cannot simply be described as food but also as art itself and an experience, an explosion of flavours never before experienced. Joaquin's menu does not actually contain any food information – simply his philosophy and the options of a light lunch, medium lunch, full lunch or children's menu. Therefore, the diners do not know what will be served each day, just the number of courses they will receive. Joaquin explained to me that he doesn't decide what will be on his menu each day until he sees what the best produce available is and then he starts to concoct his dishes. Each dish so beautiful, it was a shame to eat it and each dish has instructions on the order in which to eat it to maximise flavour and senses, even down to the pre-lunch appetizers which consisted of two olives on a skewer and a straw. We had to eat one olive, suck up the straw which provided a surprisingly strong Vermouth and then follow immediately with the second olive. I feel particularly honoured as Joaquin does not let anyone enter his kitchen ever and he not only allowed me to see where the magic takes place but also shared with me his sacred recipes. Our lunch consisted of eight courses so I have chosen my favourites for you and believe me, if you make these you will certainly impress your guests.

SWEET VERMOUTH STRAWS

Olives are an excellent source of good fats and have also been shown to reduce blood pressure and cholesterol resulting in a healthier heart. They reduce inflammation and pain in the body and are effective in fighting infections. Vermouth is actually known as a medicinal wine and been used for centuries to treat a range of ailments such as jaundice, rheumatism, anaemia and PMS. Vermouth calms an agitated stomach and increases the production of bile so aiding gallbladder and liver problems. This aperitif has a three star health rating.

INGREDIENTS FOR FOUR
PEOPLE
Prepare the day before
Cooking 10 minutes
Assembly 5 minutes

250ml Vermouth sweet and white
3 strips of gelatine
8 olives preferably stuffed with anchovy.

Soften the gelatine with cold water. Heat a little of the vermouth. Remove from the heat when hot and add the gelatine and the rest of the vermouth. Put in a tub, cover and leave in the fridge for a minimum of 12 hours.

Using a syringe (these can be purchased from any chemist), fill each straw with the vermouth mixture.

Place the olives onto a little skewer and serve together in a small glass.

Eat one olive, drink from the straw and finish with the second olive for a flavour explosion.

FRESH ASPARAGUS & CAVIAR SALAD

Asparagus is a nutrient rich food packed with antioxidant and anti-inflammatory properties. It is an excellent source of folic acid as well as vitamins A, C and K. It is a natural diuretic therefore ridding the body of excess salts and fluids. The cheese will add some fat and additional calories but also protein and calcium. This is a three star health rated dish.

INGREDIENTS FOR FOUR PEOPLE

Cooking 10 minutes

⸻

8 asparagus spears

100g cheese (pecorino or parmesan work well but you can can use literally any grateable cheese)

10g lemon caviar

Oil

Red pepper

Salt

Sauté the asparagus in a little oil until cooked (a couple of minutes each side).

Meanwhile grate the cheese. Slice the cooked asparagus and place into bowls. Surround with a little of the lemon caviar and top with the cheese.

Finish with the red pepper and a touch of salt.

MUSSELS ESCABECHE

Mussels are an excellent source of protein which is required for the functioning of every cell in the body as well as being known for muscle building and repair. They are an excellent source of selenium which boosts the immune system, the thyroid and fertility. Olives are rich in heart healthy fats and reduce pain and inflammation in the body. Garlic is a fantastic immune booster as well as promoting a healthy cardiovascular system. This dish is nutrient rich and therefore has a three star health rating.

INGREDIENTS FOR FOUR PEOPLE
Prepare the day before
Cooking 15 minutes
Assembly 5 minutes

———

20 mussels

1 clove of garlic crushed

Quarter of one lemon

Olive oil

4 pickled onions

4 small gherkins pickled

4 capers pickled

8 black olives

2 tins of mussels in escabeche
(these are easily located online)

1 lime

Gelatine – 3 sheets

250ml dry sherry

Salt

Wash the mussels well, then place in a pan with the oil, garlic and lemon. Once the shells have opened, remove from the heat and take the mussels out of the shells and place in a covered bowl. Discard any mussels which have not opened.

Open the tins of mussels and drain the liquid into a jug then add this liquid to the cooked mussels. Soften the gelatine in cold water. Heat a little of the sherry in a pan and once hot, remove from the heat. Add the gelatine then the rest of the sherry. Once mixed, place in the fridge for a minimum of 12 hours.

Joaquin served this dish in decorative tins but it can be served any way you wish. To build the dish, place five mussels in each bowl, one caper, one pickled onion, one mini gherkin and two olives. Add the sherry gelatine mixture evenly between the four dishes then finish with grated lime zest.

COCIDO MADRILEÑO
MOTHER'S STEW

This dish is definitely protein rich with the array of meats and the chickpeas too. It is also a fibre dense dish keeping everything regular and promoting a healthy digestive system. The fideo and potatoes provide energy and the cabbage not only adds an impressive amount of vitamins K and C boosting the immune system, blood clotting and bone health but it is also bursting with antioxidants and so protects the body from those harmful free radicals that cause illness, disease and premature ageing. This is a two star health rated dish.

INGREDIENTS FOR FOUR PEOPLE

It is important to soak the chickpeas overnight

Cooking 3 hours 30 minutes

Please note this dish contains chicken. Wash hands throughly when using raw poultry and ensure that you use separate chopping boards and utensils for the raw chicken to the rest of the ingredients of cooked foods.

500g dried chickpeas

125g fideo (this is in between a pasta and a noodle and very famous in Spain and readily available)

Half a chicken

200g beef ribs

200g black pudding

1 whole bone marrow

1 ham on the bone

125g pancetta unsmoked

125g smoked pancetta

There are several stages to preparing this dish so it is advisable to read through all stages prior to commencing so that the process required is fully understood.

Soak the chickpeas in water overnight. The following day once soaked, place the meats, bones and pancetta into a pressure cooker, cover with water and bring to the boil.

Rinse the chick peas and add to the boiling liquid.

Cover and leave to cook for one hour. Remove the lid, season with salt then cook for a further 12 minutes without the lid on the pan.

Remove the meats and set aside, keeping warm and save the liquid to make the soup element of this dish.

INGREDIENTS

Quarter of a cabbage shredded

4 medium potatoes, washed and chopped

2 cloves of garlic sliced

1 whole chorizo

Paprika

Salt

INGREDIENTS

300g beef, minced

Breadcrumbs from half a loaf of bread that has been soaked in water

2 cloves of garlic, chopped

A handful of pine nuts

1 egg

Pepper

Chopped parsley

A splash of olive oil

Place the chorizo in a pan of boiling salted water and cook for half an hour.

Whilst still on the heat, add the potatoes and the cabbage. (There should be just enough water to cover the contents) Once the vegetables are soft, remove the chorizo and set aside with the other cooked meats. Drain the vegetables and set aside and save the liquid.

Add a little olive oil to a frying pan and add the sliced garlic and a generous pinch of paprika. Add the drained vegetables to the pan and sauté for a few minutes.

Mix all the ingredients together well. Roll into two pieces. Roll in flour before adding to the stock in which the vegetables were cooked and cook for half an hour.

To make the fideo:
Add the fideo to the liquid that was used to cook the meats and cook according to the packet instructions. If you require additional liquid, then use the liquid from the vegetables.

Once all the elements of the dish are cooked, serve the meats, chickpeas and vegetables on a plate with a side serving of the fideo soup.

GREEK YOGHURT WITH FRESH AND DRIED BERRIES

Strawberries are packed with vitamins, fibre and antioxidants. They are low calorie and have been shown to reduce both cholesterol and blood pressure making them a true heart healthy food. One serving of strawberries also provides more vitamin C than an orange boosting collagen production and promoting a healthy immune system. Given that the creamy base of this dish is predominantly Greek yoghurt is another benefit providing added protein, less fat and calories than cream. Greek yoghurt is also packed with probiotics which is the healthy bacteria that boosts the immune system and promotes a healthy digestive system. This dish does contain some cream and does have added sugar increasing the fat and calorie content of this dessert resulting in it being a two star health rated dish.

INGREDIENTS FOR FOUR PEOPLE
Cooking 10 minutes

—⁓—

4 individual portion standard pots of Greek yoghurt or the equivalent weight in a larger pot

100g cream

16 strawberries

1 tablespoon of white sugar

Handful of cornflakes

Brown sugar

Dried strawberries

1 lime

Wash and chop the fresh strawberries then place in a bowl and cover with the white sugar.

Whip the cream until stiff then add by folding in gently to the Greek yoghurt.

Place or pipe into glass bowls a little of the yoghurt mixture, then add some fresh strawberries, some cornflakes and dried strawberries and then add a little more yoghurt mixture.

Finish with a pinch of brown sugar and a little grated lime zest.

CASA MANOLO

Passeig Maritim, 5, 46710, Daimus, Valencia

Casa Manolo is a family restaurant passed through various generations and situated on the beach in Gandia. Whilst beach restaurants are not well known for their quality of food, this restaurant really is a diamond in the sand. The meals that I was both lucky enough and honoured to cook with the owner Manuel and his wonderful team of chefs would not look out of place in any of the finest restaurants in the world, most of which cannot boast a view of golden sands and the music of the sea. Manuel explained to me that he isn't married and doesn´t have children as this restaurant is his wife, his child – his whole life – and that is clear to see within minutes of speaking with him and seeing his passion for not only the food but his staff, his customers and every part of the restaurant.

The restaurant is split into three separate sections; a more relaxed venue with smaller, lighter meals, the main restaurant which is a full elaborate menu and then the third part which again is a restaurant, but which offers more affordable and traditional everyday Spanish cuisine. All three are beautifully decorated and each have their own theme and ambience. The restaurants have a view of the open plan kitchens where the chefs can be seen busily creating the wonderful dishes from the fresh produce delivered daily from organic vegetables, to fresh fish and the finest cuts of meats. Rows of jars of exotic herbs and spices line the shelves and the large wood smoker takes pride of place at the entrance to the kitchens. Casa Manolo has an extensive choice of dishes, but I have chosen a selection of appetizers that really do look too good to eat, a starter, main course and dessert that will most certainly please your taste buds but also are visually incredible – perfect if you are looking to impress guests!

APPETIZER: MINIATURE LAMB TACOS

The tacos are baked and not fried and the lamb is an excellent source of protein as well as the minerals magnesium, iron, zinc, copper, potassium and calcium and B vitamins. This, coupled with the delicious combination of carrot, red onion and courgettes sautéed in the heart healthy olive oil, gives this starter two healthy stars. It would have been three stars but for the saturated fat content of the lamb!

INGREDIENTS FOR FOUR
PEOPLE PROVIDING TWO
TACOS EACH
Cooking 25 minutes

4 Corn tortillas
300g Cooked lamb
Salt for seasoning
1 tablespoon of Olive oil
1 Courgette
1 carrot
1 red onion

You can make your own tortillas, but for an appetizer that may be a little too time consuming and these really are fabulous anyway and super quick and simple. Heat your oven to 350°C. Place a wire rack over a baking tray. Using a cookie cutter, cut as many tacos as you require from the corn tortillas. Wrap the cut tacos in a clean damp towel and warm in the oven for only two minutes by which time they will be flexible. Remove from the oven, brush both sides with olive oil, sprinkle with salt then shape them into taco shells by placing them between the rails of the wire rack. Bake until crisp which will take between 12 to 15 minutes. These will actually keep fresh in an airtight container for up to three days.

Whilst the tortillas are crisping in the oven, prepare the delicate taco filling.

Slice the courgette and carrot into julienne strips, slice the red onion. In a small frying pan, sauté the carrot and courgette strips in a little olive oil until just cooked but still crisp. If the lamb has been cooked earlier, reheat.

Remove the tacos from the oven, fill with the lamb, top with the julienne strips of courgettes and carrots and add a couple of slices of red onion.

Quick and simple – but visually impressive and delicious!

STARTER: OCTUPUS WITH ARTICHOKE PUREE

Octopus is lean and low in calories, an excellent source of protein, B vitamins and iron. Pork is also an excellent source of protein as well as iron and magnesium, but this recipe does include the fat hence it should be eaten in moderation. Artichokes are bursting with fibre and antioxidants – thereby this dish has a two star health rating. Remove the fat and it has all three stars.

INGREDIENTS FOR FOUR PEOPLE

Cooking if using a whole octopus 3 hours 30 minutes

—⟋⟍—

200g octopus
200g pork joint with fat (crackling) still attached

For the sauce:

Salsa Española – this is a very commonly used and traditional sauce in many Spanish dishes. The recipe can be found over the page.
Grapefruit juice

For the puree:

Artichoke
Olive oil
Salt
Ground pepper

For the chips:

Artichokes
Sunflower oil

Boil the octopus in salted water. If using a whole octopus, this will take between two to three hours until it is tender. A smaller amount can be cooked in around 90 minutes. Just before serving, cut into portion size pieces and heat in some of the Salsa Espanola.

Place the pork in a roasting tin and pat dry before leaving for half an hour. During this time preheat the oven to 240°C. Score the skin with a sharp knife, rub with olive oil and season with salt and pepper. Place in the oven on a high shelf for around 25 minutes before reducing the heat to 190°C. Calculate the remaining cooking time at 35 minutes per pound but reduce the initial 25 minutes it has already cooked. No need to baste. To check the meat is cooked, insert a skewer into the thickest part and the juices should be clear. Once cooked, remove from the oven and leave to rest for 30 minutes before carving.

To make the sauce, reduce the grapefruit juice over a low heat until it has a caramel like texture. Mix with the salsa Española until you have a smooth, shiny but still fairly thick consistency. Pour into a bottle with a squeezy pouring spout.

To make the puree which can be done whilst the octopus and pork are cooking, clean the artichokes, remove the tough outer leaves and then cut into quarters. Place into a bag with a little oil, salt and

Salsa Española
Ingredients

6 mushrooms

2 onions

2 cloves of garlic

2 tablespoons of flour

3-4 tablespoons of pureed
tomatoes

1 cup of stock

Half a glass of brandy

Half a glass of red wine

Half a glass of water

Olive oil

Salt

Thyme

Rosemary

pepper, then seal and place in a pan to steam for 15 minutes. Remove from the bag and puree.

To make the chips which again can be done whilst the octopus and pork are cooking, again wash an artichoke, remove the tough outer leaves until you reach the lighter yellow leaves. Using a mandolin, slice the artichoke into thin slices. Heat a little oil in a pan and sauté the slices until golden and crispy.

Salsa Española
Chop the garlic and onions and brown them in a pan with the olive oil. Season with salt, add the mushrooms, a couple of sprigs of thyme and rosemary. Add the flour and cook for one minute before adding the pureed tomatoes. Add the brandy, red wine, water and stock and bring to the boil. Once boiling, reduce the heat and simmer for a further 25 minutes, removing any foam during the cooking process. Allow to cool, then pass through a sieve, leaving a thick smooth sauce.

To plate up:
Using flat white plates, squeeze a line across the centre of the plate of the sauce then tip the plate until the sauce runs to one side creating a teardrop effect. Along the line of the sauce, spread a generous line of the artichoke puree before placing two portions of the octopus that has been heated in the salsa onto the puree at each end. In the middle place a slice of the pork and crackling – remember this is a starter, so keep the portions delicate. In between each item place the sautéed artichoke chips. Casa Manolo also added the skins of some baby onions before garnishing with beetroot leaves.

SLOW COAL GRILLED TUNA WITH CARROT CREAM AND SALSA PERIGEAUX

Tuna is rich in omega 3 fatty acids which have been proven to aid healthy cholesterol levels. It is also an excellent source of potassium which has been shown to reduce blood pressure, so it really is a super heart healthy food. It is low in fat yet rich in protein and immune boosting nutrients. The carrot cream is rich in fibre and antioxidants and whilst the salsa Perigeaux does contain butter and cream, this is used in very small quantities in this dish and so it has a full three star healthy dish rating.

INGREDIENTS FOR FOUR
PEOPLE
Cooking 35 minutes

Please note that this recipe
suggests cooking over charcoal.
If using this method please ensure
it is done outside.

—⁓—

800g joint of tuna

For the carrot cream:
200g carrot
50g orange juice

For the Salsa Perigeaux:
290g salsa Española
6g thyme
12g parmesan
20g butter
25ml Vinegar de Modena
30g cream
4 baby corn

Sorrel leaves to garnish

Place the tuna joint to cook over coals as in
a barbeque and close the lid – this will take
approximately 30 minutes. Season with a little oil
and salt prior to cooking.

To make the salsa, place the salsa Española in a
pan and heat until it reduces slightly before adding
the thyme and butter. Heat a little longer before
adding the vinegar of Modena, then the cheese
and finally the cream. Stir for one minute then
reserve.

To make the carrot cream, boil the carrots until
soft, drain and puree. Add the orange juice, a little
salt, then place into a piping bag.

A couple of minutes before the tuna is ready, add
the baby corn to the grill to char.

To plate up:
Remove the tuna joint and break into three steaks
placing them in a triangle on the plate. Using the
piping bag, pipe generous dots of the carrot cream
around the edges of the plate and also onto the tuna
steaks. Slice the baby corn into bite size pieces and
arrange them on top of the carrot cream. Drizzle the
whole plate with the salsa and garnish with the sorrel
leaves. If you want a colour contrast to the carrot
cream, you can also make a courgette cream.

FROZEN MELON AND YOGHURT, CUCUMBER AND BASIL

As far as desserts go, in terms of healthiness this really is quite impressive. The combination of melon, mint and cucumber – low in calories, virtually fat free, bursting with vitamins and minerals – will boost digestion, reduce inflammation and even reduce stress. The yoghurt and milk add calcium and protein, but the added sugar does reduce the health rating of this dish to two stars.

INGREDIENTS FOR FOUR
PEOPLE
Part of this recipe must be made at least twelve hours in advance or the day prior.
Cooking 35 minutes

400g melon
Handful of blackberries and blueberries to decorate
Mint leaves to decorate

For the frozen yoghurt mixture:
500g natural yoghurt
500ml milk
Juice of 1 lime
50g cream
250g sugar

For the minted cucumber:
200g water
50g fresh mint
50g sugar
250g cucumber

Puree the melon well and freeze for at least several hours or overnight.

To make the yoghurt, place all the ingredients into a food processor or blender and mix until smooth. Place in the freezer for at least several hours or overnight.

To make the minted cucumber, make a mint infusion by pouring boiling water over the mint leaves, add the sugar, stir until dissolved and leave for 15 minutes. Drain the liquid and chill. Peel the cucumber and cut into long strips of around 10cm. Place into a bowl with the mint infusion and chill.

For the cream, place the milk, cream and seeds from the vanilla pod into a pan and bring to the boil before sieving the liquid. Place to one side. In a bowl mix the cornflour with the egg yolks then add the milk and cream mixture. Place over a medium heat and stir until the mixture thickens. Once it has thickened, remove from the heat and place into a blender or food processor and add the butter. Mix until smooth before pouring into a piping bag.

To plate up, firstly place several tablespoons

For the cream:
500g milk
500g cream
1 vanilla pod
80g cornflour
200g (around 11) egg yolks
180g butter
200g sugar

of the minted cucumber in the base of a wide bowl. Cover the left side of the cucumber with several scoops of the frozen melon and then the right side with several scoops of the frozen yoghurt. Pipe the cream around the outside of the bowl before placing three to four blackberries and blueberries and mint leaves to garnish the dish.

HELADOS LLINARES

Plaza de la Reina, 6, 46001, Valencia

Well, my daughter Isabella and I were certainly in for a treat when we had the opportunity to visit the factory where all the ice cream that supplies a large number of Llinares Ice Cream stores across Spain, is produced. Helados Llinares is a family run business spanning four generations now. Despite bringing the company into the modern era, they have certainly not lost any of their attention to detail, quality of product despite a huge increase in the quantity of production or reduced the quality of their ingredients. Whilst many current ice cream stores and brands produce a wide range of products by simply adding different artificial flavours to their regular base mixture, at Helados Llinares every single flavour is made using real fresh authentic ingredients.

On the day we visited the production warehouse, they were making strawberry and turron (almost like an almond nougat which is extremely famous and popular in Spain) flavours and Isabella and I were involved in the process of washing, pureeing and even removing the seeds from a rather large quantity of strawberries before adding this mixture to the milk base. We watched as bars of turron were reduced to a thick creamy puree which was then added to the

machines busily stirring the mixtures. Currently producing over seventy flavours in this one factory – a quick, cold visit to the storage unit which is a cool minus 26 degrees was 'better than Charlie and the Chocolate Factory' according to Isabella who ran around excitedly reading the names of the all the flavours meticulously stacked metres high, with flavours ranging from After Eight, Donut, Kinder, Oreo, Vanilla Cookie, Vanilla Bourbon, Chocolate, Dulce De Leche, Forrest Fruits, Tutti Frutti, and fifty-nine flavours more. Felix, one of the owners of the company, explained to me that they slightly change the recipes in winter and summer as in summer their customers want a colder more refreshing ice cream yet in winter, they require a denser, creamier product. It is a subtle change but most definitely worth it.

While large machines dispense the finished product, at Helados Llinares these are still placed into the tubs by hand, something else we were able to participate in – I actually think I could have found my talent as I produced some pretty impressive finishes on my tubs! Above the factory where today's ice creams are produced is a wonderful museum of all their various ice cream machines, scoops, stalls, bikes with ice cream tubs on the back dating right back to when their grandparents made their very first ice creams, cutting blocks of ice with a pick and hand stirring the mixture until frozen. It was most definitely a labour of love and after spending several hours with this wonderful family, I have no doubt that it still is. If you are ever visiting Spain, then I highly recommend you search for your nearest Helados Llinares shop so that you too can experience one of the finest ice creams I have ever tasted. Now to bring a little of the famous Spanish ice cream to your own home, Felix has kindly shared the secrets of a couple of his popular flavours and provided me with the recipes for you to recreate at home. Enjoy!

HOMEMADE FRESH STRAWBERRY ICE CREAM (60 PER CENT FRUIT)

Ice cream is rarely described as a health food – however these two recipes do still have a wide range of nutritional benefits. The strawberries make up 60% of the ingredients of this recipe providing vitamin C and plenty of potassium thereby boosting the immune system and even brain function. Strawberries are also rich in flavonoids which can reduce inflammation in the body. The milk provides calcium for healthy teeth and bones and it has also been proven that drinking milk increases the absorption of vital nutrients. Unfortunately, the added sugar and glucose syrup result in a one star health rating.

INGREDIENTS FOR EIGHT SERVINGS
Cooking 50 minutes

500ml whole milk
500ml fresh cream
225g sugar
500g fresh strawberries
2 teaspoons vanilla extract

Wash the strawberries and puree using a blender before passing through a sieve to remove any large seeds.

Place the milk, cream, vanilla extract and sugar into a saucepan and heat on low until the sugar has dissolved.

Add the pureed strawberries before transferring into an ice cream maker. This usually takes around 25-30 minutes but depends of the brand and size of machine.

Once completed, decorate with sliced strawberries before serving – delicious (and a little healthy too)!

TURRON ICE CREAM

Almonds are rich in antioxidants thus protecting the body from harmful free radicals, diseases and premature ageing. They are rich in vitamin E and magnesium and have been shown to be effective in lowering both blood pressure and cholesterol. Cinnamon is a natural anti-inflammatory, prevents infections, is also beneficial in reducing blood pressure and cholesterol whilst honey is also anti-bacterial, provides a boost to the immune system and also aids a healthy digestive system. Unfortunately, given the added sugar, this ice cream also has a one star health rating.

Turron translates as 'nougat' but it really is nothing like the nougat we know in the UK. It is really popular in Spain especially during the festive season where it is often given as a gift and adorns the shelves of every single shop. It is actually made from almonds – like a sweet almond candy – and whilst there are conflicting rumours, it is thought that turron was created by the Arabs when they were looking for a food that would keep for long periods yet could provide an excellent source of nutrients that their armies could transport with them. The word turron actually derives from 'torrat' which means a mix of honey, dried fruits and nuts cooked directly on the fire. So to make this very special ice cream we must first make the turron – this mixture will provide 500g turron, so enough for the ice cream and a little left over for decoration.

Cooking 1 hour

TURRON INGREDIENTS
300g ground almonds
Powdered cinnamon – quantity adjusted to taste
100g sugar
200g honey
1 egg white
Zest of one lemon

Whisk the egg white, place the sugar and honey in a pan and stir over a medium heat until they form a thick mixture. Remove from the heat, add the egg white and stir well until all the lumps have disappeared and the mixture has changed to a lighter colour – this will take around ten minutes.

Add the lemon zest and cinnamon before stirring in the ground almonds. Stir well until combined. At this point we would normally transfer the mixture into a container lined with greaseproof paper, press it down really tightly before leaving to set and harden a little. However, as we are using this mixture to combine with the ice cream, we actually need it in its 'unset' state.

ICE CREAM INGREDIENTS FOR 10 PORTIONS

1210ml whole milk
300g sugar
80g Inverted sugar
400g turron

Heat the milk and sugars in a pan until the sugar has dissolved before adding the turron mixture and pouring into an ice cream maker – again this should take around 30 minutes but will depend on the size of the machine and the brand.

Place the remaining turron mixture into a container lined with greaseproof paper, press down hard and leave to set. This is lovely added to the finished ice cream or as a treat on the side.

ASKUA

Askua, Carrer de Felip Maria Garin, 4, 46021, Valencia

Askua is a traditional Spanish restaurant hidden behind a most plain exterior close to the famous Mestalla Stadium – the home of Valencia Football Club and the reason that I ended up living in Spain. If you didn't know about this wonderful hidden gem, then you would walk straight past it completely unaware of the incredible food and ambience behind the façade that resembles nothing more than a small house.

Askua has been serving traditional in-season only food for more than 20 years. Both the kitchen and dining room are relatively small but modern and pretty cool! The staff are like a family and I was lucky enough to spend a day with them and see just how they prepare some of their most popular dishes. As they only serve in-season food, the menu changes from season to season but fish and meat remain the most popular dishes. The real wood grill in the kitchen was incredible to watch and made me want one for my own kitchen when I experienced the food it was capable of producing. Produce of the highest quality, simple but exquisite food, clean and simple surroundings, chefs that take extreme pride in their work and put a great deal of love into the food that they prepare and an owner that clearly, after more than two decades, has not lost any of his passion for taking great care of his customers and ensuring that every single moment spent in his restaurant is an enjoyable one makes Askua a restaurant to visit without doubt. I want to share with you four recipes that we cooked during my visit, each one simple, very traditional Spanish but delicious. I hope that you enjoy them as much as I did.

GUISANTES LAGRIMA
GREEN CAVIAR

This actually translates as peas' tears and is produced only in one part of Northern Spain and only during two months of the year, so it really is a delicacy. You may have to work a little harder to source these for your dinner party! Rich in protein, fibre and macro nutrients, boosting energy the immune system, heart health, digestion and contributing to healthy bones. This dish most certainly deserves its full three star health rating.

INGREDIENTS FOR
FOUR PEOPLE
Cooking times 2 minutes

100g guisantes lagrima
1 tablespoon of olive oil
Salt to season

Very simply, heat the olive oil, add the green caviar and saute only for a minute or so until they change colour slightly. Serve in plain white bowls.

The barbel of a fish is the slender organ near the mouth – not every type of fish has them and I have been told by the chefs of Askua that the barbels of the hake are the very best, especially for this dish. I suggest you speak to your fishmonger in order to purchase these as they are readily available in Spain but probably less so in the UK. This dish is amazing – what can be created through few ingredients but a specific process of cooking with simple yet delicious ingredients.

HAKE BARBELS PIL PIL

Garlic has long been used for its medicinal purposes and for good reason. It has been shown to boost the immune system, lower both cholesterol and blood pressure, detoxify the body and even boost athletic performance. Chilli pepper has been shown to be an effective natural pain reliever, also boosts heart health, promotes intestinal health and can fight infections. This dish is calorific given the large amount of olive oil used, but given the heart and brain benefits, its immune boosting ability as well as olive oil being a natural anti-inflammatory, this dish still achieves a three star health rating.

INGREDIENTS TO SERVE FOUR
To share served with warm bread
Cooking 45 minutes

10 barbels
1 clove of garlic, sliced
1½ chilli peppers, chopped finely
Olive oil
Salt to season

Cover the bottom of a pan with olive oil (around 0.5cm deep) – preferably a double handled pan, given the process used for cooking this dish. Add the garlic and chilli pepper and heat on medium.

Once the garlic has started to brown, remove from the heat to prevent it burning. Leave to cool a little before adding the barbels, skin side down. Place back on the heat for a couple of minutes then remove again and with hands on both handles shake the pan in circular movements creating a swirling of the contents. Continue for a couple of minutes until you notice the oil starting to thicken and change to a whitish colour.

Place back on the heat for a couple of minutes then repeat the process. Continue with this routine three or four times until the liquid that was in the pan resembles a mayonnaise and is completely white and thickened. Serve in the pan with good quality bread to soak up all the delicious sauce.

FINEST AGED FILLET OF BEEF

Beef is an excellent source of the amino acid L-Carnitine which plays an important role in transporting fat in order to be used as a source of fuel for our body. It has also been shown to be effective in promoting heart health and weight loss. Beef is also rich in the antioxidant Glutathione which prevents illness, disease, premature ageing and boosts the immune system. It is a wonderful source of protein required to repair and build muscle, bone and cartilage. It is also a fantastic source of minerals especially selenium and zinc. As long as red meat is not eaten every single day, this dish has a three star health rating.

INGREDIENTS TO SERVE TWO PEOPLE

Cooking for a medium meat 15 minutes.

Please note it is mentioned here that the meat is cooked over charcoal. If using this method please ensure that this is done outdoors.

—⁓—

400g aged fillet of beef on the bone

Salt

Season generously with large crystals of salt and place on the grill – we cooked in the restaurant on open flames from charcoal so the meat took on a real smoky flavour. This would work wonderfully on a barbeque.

Very simply grill to your preference on both sides. Remove from the grill, slice off the bone then slice the steak into strips. Season with more salt before serving. In Spain they return the bone to the grill whilst slicing the steak then serve the bone on the side – which given the size of it, I have to admit looks pretty impressive!

ESGARRAT

Esgarrat is a very popular and traditional starter or Almuerzo in Spain and is available in many restaurants, cafes and bars. Really simple to make yet delicious! Cod is a low calorie source of protein rich in heart healthy omega 3 fatty acids as well as Vitamins B12 and B6. Red peppers are bursting with vitamin C and antioxidants therefore boosting the immune system and fighting infection and disease. Research has also shown that red peppers boost the metabolism. This is absolutely a three star healthy dish.

INGREDIENTS FOR
FOUR PEOPLE
Cooking 35 minutes
Please note that the peppers in this recipe need sufficient time to cool before serving

Two red peppers
240g Strips of smoked and chilled cod
Olive oil

Cut the peppers in half and place on a roasting tray. Put into a pre-heated oven at 200°C for around 25 minutes until the peppers are a little charred and soft. Remove from the oven and when cooled a little remove the skins and slice into long strips – leave to cool.

Once cooled completely, place the strips of pepper into a bowl with the strips of cod and mix with a little olive oil – season if required.

Place a metal, bottomless mould onto a plate and fill with the mixture, then carefully remove the mould leaving the Esgarrat beautifully placed. Drizzle the plate with a little olive oil and garnish with fresh herbs.

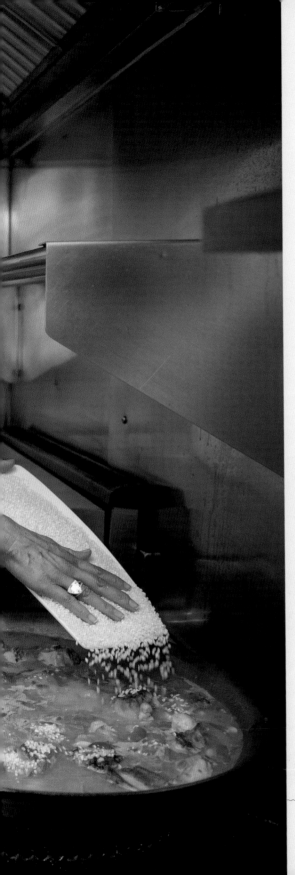

PAELLA VALENCIANA

Paella is such a wonderful dish providing a wonderful mix of protein, carbohydrates and heart healthy fats, filled with vegetables and rich in fibre. The paprika provides an antioxidant boost whilst the saffron has anti-cancer properties and has been shown to boost brain function. Three star health rating.

INGREDIENTS – TO SERVE SIX PEOPLE
Cooking 1 hour and 20 minutes
Please note this dish contains chicken. Wash hands thoroughly when using raw poultry and ensure that you use separate chopping boards and utensils for the raw chicken and the rest of the ingredients and cooked foods.

One whole chicken cut into sections or one whole rabbit cut into sections or you can use half of each

40g pureed tomatoes
500g green beans
500g garrofon (Lima beans)
10g paprika
Water – approximately one litre
Oil
600g paella rice
3g saffron

Heat a large paella pan with the base covered with olive oil and add the chicken and rabbit pieces. Season with salt.

These will take around 20-30 minutes to cook through. Once cooked, add the tomatoes, green beans and the broad beans as well as the paprika and stir well. Allow to brown for a minute or two before adding the water and saffron.

Add a little more salt then bring to the boil and leave to simmer for 25 minutes until the green beans are cooked and the broad beans are soft. Add the rice and leave to cook for a further 20 minutes until all the liquid has been absorbed and the rice is perfectly cooked. You may wish to add more oil as the rice is cooking and stir occasionally to prevent the rice sticking to the pan. Traditional Paella Valenciana is served dry and browned around the edges – much dryer and crispier than a risotto texture.

CINNAMON CREAM WITH WARM CHOCOLATE SAUCE

The milk in this recipe provides calcium and some protein and the egg yolks are a rare food source of vitamin D as well as boosting cognitive and memory function and heart health. That said, this recipe is also high in fat, sugar and calories and so it has a TREAT rating.

INGREDIENTS FOR
Cooking 35 minutes
Please note that this dessert needs to be refrigerated for a minimum of two hours prior to serving

---

1ltr double cream – semi whipped so that it is slightly fluffy and forming soft not stiff peaks

Crushed biscuits

8 eggs with the yolks and whites separated

200ml milk

15g ground cinnamon

350g sugar

18g gelatine

For the chocolate sauce:
200g chocolate
200ml cream
300ml milk

To make the cinnamon cream, place the yolks of the eight eggs in a pan and add the 200ml of milk. Heat over a low heat whilst stirring until you obtain a light cream texture before adding the gelatine. Add the cream and the cinnamon and mix. Whip the egg whites until forming soft peaks and add to the mixture with the sugar and stir well. Place bottomless moulds onto a plate and fill the bases around an inch deep with the crushed biscuits. Press down well. Pour the cinnamon cream mixture into the moulds and then refrigerate for at least two hours.

To make the chocolate sauce – melt the chocolate in a bowl over a pan of boiling water, then add the cream and the milk and stir well.

To serve, remove the moulds from the cinnamon cream and pour the warm chocolate sauce around the base to fill the plate and serve extra chocolate sauce in a jug on the side. Garnish with berries and caramelized pecans.

KAYMUS

Kaymus, Avenida del Mestre Rodrigo, 44, 46015, Valencia

Kaymus is one of my favourite restaurants in Valencia, simple and modern and serving the most amazing food. It was opened in 2008 by Nacho Romero who is pretty much a celebrity in Spain. Nacho worked in some of the best restaurants before finally realising his dream and opening his own. Only two years after opening, he received a most prestigious award for gastronomy and in 2012 Kaymus was nominated for a Michelin Star.

Working in the kitchen with Nacho was an incredible experience, the preparation, the organization, the finest ingredients, the innovative recipes and I was most honoured to have had the opportunity as this is a man in demand whose working day begins at 8am and finishes at 1am every day of the week! The skill and dedication of every single staff member is incredible and I fully enjoyed having a behind the scenes view of what goes into putting their fabulous food onto the plates for their most loyal diners. Nacho was kind enough to teach me how to prepare one of their popular starters, a 'special' Kaymus paella and the most delicious yet simple dessert. I am excited to share them with you but even more excited to recreate them in my own kitchen.

SMOKED COD CROQUETTES

The ingredients in this dish are simply wonderful. The low calorie, omega 3 rich cod, the anti-bacterial, anti-inflammatory garlic, the eggs rich in vitamin D and protein, the antioxidant rich paprika and the detoxifying, immune and digestion boosting onions. However, these are fried and therefore are a two star health rated dish.

INGREDIENTS FOR 20
CROQUETTES ALLOWING
TWO PER PERSON
Cooking 50 minutes

3 large potatoes boiled (the size of a jacket potato)

400g smoked cod

1 tablespoon minced garlic

1 tablespoon of minced cooked onion

1 tablespoon paprika

3 egg yolks

3 egg whites

Boil the potatoes in their skins then when soft squeeze them through a sieve to provide a soft fine potato.

Place in a bowl and add the onion, garlic, paprika, cod and egg yolks and mix well. Beat the egg whites with a little water.

Form the potato mixture into croquette shapes, soak for a moment in the egg white mixture before frying in a well oiled pan (sunflower oil works well and it has to be really hot) until golden brown on all sides.

CUTTLEFISH, CAULIFLOWER, GARLIC AND SMOKED PANCETTA WITH RICE

Cuttlefish is low in fat, a good source of protein, an excellent source of iron and selenium as well as B vitamins. Cauliflower is actually thought to be one of the healthiest foods on the planet, boosting heart and brain health. It is a natural anti-inflammatory, aids the body in its detoxification process, has been shown to prevent cancer and even prevent weight gain. Garlic is a super heart healthy food and boosts the immune system; paprika provides an antioxidant boost. Pancetta is the indulgence in this dish being high in fat and calories so if you want to be super healthy you can exclude it although it is not used here in very large quantities resulting in a three star health rating.

INGREDIENTS FOR FOUR
PEOPLE
Cooking 30 minutes

———

1 whole cuttlefish, skin removed
and cut into pieces

400g paella rice

Half a cauliflower cut into even
sized pieces

6 cloves garlic

80g smoked pancetta chopped

1 tablespoon paprika

2 tablespoons of pureed
tomatoes

1 tablespoon of minced garlic

Fish stock

Heat a few tablespoons of oil in a paella pan and add the cuttlefish, garlic cloves, cauliflower and pancetta and sauté for a few minutes before adding the minced garlic, paprika and tomato.

Add the rice and cook for a minute or two.

Add a generous amount of stock to cover all the ingredients and simmer. Cook for around 18-20 minutes until all the stock has been absorbed and the rice is dry (you may need to add more stock during this cooking process).

SWEET CARAMEL CHEESECAKE

The milk in this dish does bring some health benefits but on the whole it is high in fat, sugar and calories resulting in it having a TREAT rating.

INGREDIENTS FOR TWENTY PORTIONS

Cooking 25 minutes

Please note that this dessert must be refrigerated for a minimum of two hours prior to serving but can be prepared in advance and stored in the fridge

―∿―

150g sugar

400g Philadelphia cheese

500ml milk

500ml cream

2 sachets of cuajada – this is actually a product I have only ever seen in Spain. It is available on the internet or it can be substituted by gelatine or even agar agar.

A couple of packets of biscuits of your choice but digestives work well.

Liquid Caramel (shop bought or homemade)

Cover the base and side of a rectangle baking pan with plenty of liquid caramel. Mix all the remaining ingredients except the cookies in a bowl then place into a pan over a medium heat and bring to the boil stirring continuously.

Strain the mixture before pouring over the caramel in the baking pan. Allow to cool slightly.

Place the biscuits into a sealable food bag and crush with a rolling pin. Pour the crushed biscuits over the mixture and place in the fridge for a minimum of a couple of hours.

To serve, turn the pan over onto a plate.

MARINA BEACH CLUB

Marina Beach Club, Carrer Marina Real Juan Carlos 1, S/N, 46011, Valencia

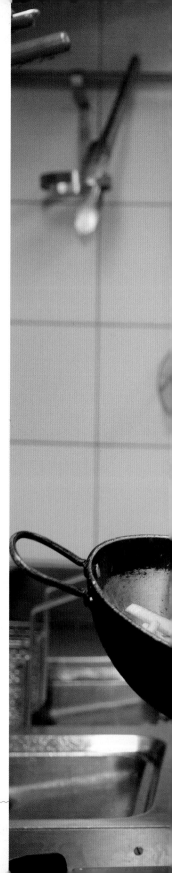

We are regular visitors to the restaurant at Marina Beach Club which can only be described as uber cool from the modern architecture of the building, to the HUGE screen playing music videos all day long, to the live DJ, to the gorgeous swimming pool, to the beautiful clientele and then to the fabulous food. Believe me, this is the place to be and it is bustling with people from opening until closing – many of them celebrities. The head chef is Sergio Giraldo and when I first met him, I was taken back at just how young he was taking into account his achievements and position within the Marina Beach Club group.

Sergio started work at the age of just 14 in a restaurant called Echaurren which holds two Michelin Stars. At the age of 17 he won an award for having the most promise in Spain out of all the upcoming chefs. He continued his studies alongside chef Martin Berasategui – holder of eight Michelin Stars and later Pedro Subijana – holder of three Michelin Stars. After managing his own kitchens in various top restaurants for several years, he accepted the position as executive chef and menu creator for the group that owns Marina Beach Club along with two other top restaurants. I was both thrilled and honoured to spend a day with Sergio in his extremely busy kitchen to see just what goes into creating the wonderful dishes that we enjoy eating. Whilst many of the dishes that they create are extremely elaborate and complex, those that I am sharing with you are wonderful yet simple to recreate in your own kitchen.

STEAK TARTARE WITH FROZEN MUSTARD ICE CREAM

This dish contains a wide array of ingredients resulting in a broad spectrum of nutrients. Mustard boasts some pretty impressive health benefits from lowering cholesterol and preventing infection to relieving pain and promoting digestive and skin health. Capers provide fibre, vitamin K and iron whilst anchovies are rich in omega 3 fatty acids, boost heart, skin, eye and bone health and aid tissue and cell repair. Beef is an excellent source of the amino acid L-Carnitine which plays an important role in transporting fat in order to be used as a source of fuel for our body. It has also been shown to be effective in promoting heart health and weight loss. Beef is also rich in the antioxidant Glutathione which prevents illness, disease, premature ageing and boosts the immune system. It is a wonderful source of protein required to repair and build muscle, bone and cartilage. The egg yolks add some vital vitamin D. However, the mustard ice cream does add calories, fat and sugar to this dish resulting in a one star health rating.

INGREDIENTS FOR
FOUR PEOPLE

Cooking 1 hour

Please note the mustard ice cream is best prepared the day before and left in the fridge overnight.

For the dressing

8 egg yolks

50g anchovy oil

25g wholegrain mustard

20g American mustard

10ml Lea and Perrins sauce

2 cooked egg yolks (passed through a sieve to ensure they are extra fine)

Black pepper

20ml HP sauce

50ml olive oil

Six drops of tabasco sauce

The vinegar from a jar of capers – the quantity required to make the perfect consistency. Note this sauce should be dense.

Put the egg yolk in a bowl, add the mustards,
the cooked egg yolks and mix well with a whisk.
Continue adding the remaining ingredients except
the vinegar of capers, leave this until last and add the
quantity required for a thick but smooth consistency.
Season with salt before pouring into a bottle.

For the mustard ice cream

50g of grained mustard

4 eggs

1l cream

80g sugar

100g food stabilizer such as
pectin or guar gum

For the meat

640g good quality beef

2 shallots

1 gherkin

5 white or brown anchovies

1 egg white

2 spoonsful of capers

Heat the cream, the food stablilizer and the sugar until boiling point, beat the eggs and the mustard then add to the cream mixture. Heat until it reaches 80 degrees then remove from the heat allow to cool then refrigerate for a minimum of 12 hours. This can then be put through a butter churner, an ice cream machine or placed in the freezer until thick but not frozen through.

Chop the meat finely until it is minced removing any fat. Chop the remaining ingredients finely also. Place the meat and half of the remaining ingredients into a bowl and using your hands mix well.

At Beach Club Marina they used a gorgeous homemade crisp bread as a base for this dish.

To plate up, add some of the egg yolk to the plate and sprinkle with capers. Place the crisp bread into the centre of the plate. Place the minced beef mixture on top of the crisp bread. Top this with more of the chopped gherkin and shallot mixture before topping with a large tablespoon of the mustard ice cream. Place a bread stick on top to decorate.

PAN SEARED TUNA STEAK WITH STIR FRIED VEGETABLES AND BASIL AIOLI

Nutritionally this is a fabulous dish. The omega rich tuna, the superfood and powerful anti-bacterial heart healthy garlic, wasabi is rich in fibre, protein, vitamins and minerals with cancer fighting properties and boosting heart health as well as aiding gut health and reducing arthritis symptoms. The sweet peas, baby corn and asparagus add further fibre, nutrients and antioxidants. A three star health rating.

INGREDIENTS FOR FOUR PEOPLE
Cooking 15 minutes

Please not that the dressing and aiolil can be made in advance

—

Four thick tuna steaks

For the dressing:
200g soy sauce

200g rice wine

5g wasabi

25g sushisu (sushi seasoning)

5g gelatine

Mix together all the ingredients and place into a thermomix and thicken with the gelatine. Set aside.

For the aioli
Basil

50g egg yolk

8 cloves of preserved garlic

200g garlic oil

Freshly squeezed lemon juice

Salt

Puree the garlic with the basil and egg yolk. Continue emulsifying with the oil then add the lemon juice and salt. Place into a bottle with a pouring spout.

Boil some peas, baby corn and wild asparagus for a couple of minutes then set aside.

Sear the tuna briefly on both sides and during this process pour over some of the soy dressing. Place into the oven with a little more dressing and bake for only 4-5 minutes covered at 185°C.

During the last two minutes of this baking process, place the cooked vegetables into a hot frying pan with some olive oil and sauté for a couple of minutes until hot.

To plate up:
Place some of the aioli decoratively onto a dark plate (it stands out more). Place the vegetables into the centre of the plate and top with the tuna sliced. Pour over a little more of the dressing and garnish with some red swiss chard leaves.

FRIED ICE CREAM

This dish is both beautiful and delicious but in terms of health star rating, this is rated as a TREAT!

INGREDIENTS FOR FOUR PEOPLE
Cooking 15 minutes

—⁓—

8 Balls of ice cream of desired flavour

For the batter:
250g Japanese tempura flour

180g water (cold)

2 egg yolks

2 ice cubes

30g sugar

Heat some sunflower oil in a pan to around 200°C.

Mix together the flour and the sugar. In a separate bowl beat the egg yolks then add the water. Tip the liquid mixture into the flour mixture, add the ice cubes and mix with your fingers – it will be quite thick.

Take the balls of ice cream, straight from the freezer, roll in the batter mixture, then fry quickly just until crispy and slightly golden. Remove from the oil and place onto kitchen paper to absorb any excess oil.

Place into the centre of a plate and drizzle with a little honey and sprinkle with brown sugar.

LA LOLA

La Lola, Pujada Del Toleda, 8, 46001, Valencia

I love it when I come across a hidden gem, something or somewhere you would never find by chance, that only the locals or those 'in the know' have knowledge of. That is exactly what I found when I was told that I just had to visit the restaurant La Lola for my book. I could have spoken with Jesus (the owner) for hours as he has had a most interesting life and is so passionate about what he does, it is impossible not to hang on his every word.

After returning from working in London in 2002, Jesus decided to open La Lola (down the tiniest quiet street) serving only the finest fresh meats and fish alongside live flamenco music and in a modern take on a flamenco decorated dining room – a little Art Deco! As its reputation and popularity grew amongst the locals, business people working in the city and tourists, so did the demand for the traditional rice dishes and paella so these too were added to the menu. Its long-standing client base has resulted in some of its most popular dishes remaining on the menu for fifteen years whilst other dishes change with the seasons and availability of the finest produce. Just twelve months ago, Jesus decided to open the La Lola deli, serving a wide range of 'simple' dishes such as the famous Jamon Ibericos (which he attempted to teach me to carve – which was extremely difficult to do I would like to add), olives, tortillas, croquettes, cheeses, anchovies, salads and all served with the finest oils and a range of wines. Entering the kitchen with his team of chefs was a pleasure as I watched them create masterpieces with such attention to the finest details down to where the petal garnish was placed. During this process, I have quickly learned that to be a chef is a vocation, long hours, stressful working environments, heat … but every single chef I have met has told me with a smile on their face that they love it – and that has been apparent in every single dish I have seen them create. Every dish at La Lola is innovative and fun but both exquisite and beautiful at the same time. I am looking forward to returning to try out more of their famous dishes soon!

WATERMELON GAZPACHO

Cleansing, refreshing, detoxing, immune boosting – this dish has it all, bursting with vitamins, minerals and antioxidants. Both the tomatoes and watermelon are rich in lycopene which is one of the most powerful antioxidants in the world helping the body fight infection and disease. Watermelon is actually 92 per cent water, making this a super hydrating dish and the onions promote a healthy immune system, boost gut health and digestions and provide a natural pain relief. Healthy never tasted so good. A three star health rating.

INGREDIENTS FOR 15 PEOPLE
Cooking 15 minutes
Please note the mandarins in this dish must be frozen once prepared and the gazpacho must be chilled after preparing prior to serving so leave sufficent time

———

1kg tomatoes
250g chopped onion
1 whole watermelon
1 green pepper
1 red pepper
180g cucumber
1 dessertspoon of olive oil
1 dessertspoon cider vinegar
Salt and pepper to season
2 Mandarins

Firstly, blend and freeze the mandarins – these can be placed into ice cube trays for ease of use and uniform in size.

Wash all the vegetables. Chop the peppers, cucumber, tomatoes and the watermelon (reserving a little watermelon for the finished dish) and place into a powerful blender.

Add the oil, vinegar, minced onion and a little salt and pepper and blend well. Pass through a sieve and chill well.

Serve in wide bowls with a ball of watermelon, a portion of frozen mandarin, a drizzle of vinegar de Modena and garnish with a little watercress.

A LOG OF FOIE GRAS WITH PRALINE AND BLACK TOASTED SESAME SEEDS

Foie gras is rich and decadent and yet high in fat; however, when eaten in moderation it actually has some health benefits. The fats in foie gras are good fats helping to lower cholesterol. Black pepper is rich in the minerals magnesium, phosphorus, calcium, potassium and iron as well as having a high fibre content. It aids digestion and also assists in breaking down fat cells. That said, this remains a dish to be eaten occasionally and has a one star health rating.

INGREDIENTS FOR FOUR PEOPLE

Cooking 15 minutes

Please note that you need to allow time to chill this prior to serving

—◦◦◦—

4 portions foie gras

4g ground black pepper

136ml brandy

2 slices of white bread

1 tablespoon of sesame seeds

4g sweetcorn

2g sugar

8g diced chives

4 dessertspoon praline (caramelized nuts)

Place the foie gras, brandy, salt, black pepper and praline into a thermomix – set at 37°C and at a speed of 2/3 until it forms a creamy paste. Remove and form into a log. Each log should weigh around 50g. Place in the fridge to chill.

Take the bread and sprinkle with sesame seeds before rolling with a rolling pin to flatten and squash the seeds into the bread. Toast lightly before cutting into a rectangle just larger than the foie log.

When ready to serve, place the toast on a plate and top with the foie log, sprinkle with the sugar and using a blow torch, caramelize the log. Sprinkle with chopped praline, chives and pipe some pureed sweetcorn at the side.

Serve with some extra slices of the toasted sesame bread.

BEEF MEDALLIONS WITH POTATO DISCS AND A RICH RED WINE SAUCE

The 'gravy' in this dish is a powerhouse of nutrients. Garlic, leeks and onions all providing antibacterial properties and boosting heart, digestive and eye health and the immune system. Red wine is rich in anti-oxidants reducing inflammation in the body; the polyphenols protect the heart and red wine has been shown to balance blood sugar levels, boost brain function and strengthen the immune system. Beef is a wonderful source of protein aiding the building and repair of muscles, bones and cartilage. This dish has a two star health rating.

INGREDIENTS FOR UP TO
TEN PEOPLE
Cooking 3 hours

—⁓—

2 kg beef medallions

1 ltr of red wine

500g carrots

500g onion

Two leeks

1kg potatoes

50ml olive oil

1 vanilla pod

2 cloves of garlic

Thyme

Salt and pepper to season

Brush the beef with olive oil and set aside. Chop the carrots, onions and leeks and place in a pan with a little oil and with salt and pepper, thyme and the garlic. Cook until caramelized and softened, then puree with a blender.

Place the pureed mixture into a pan, add the beef, wine and water to cover and simmer for two hours until the meat is tender and the sauce has thickened.

Peel the potatoes and then slice into circular strips around 1cm thick. Place these onto an oiled baking tray, brush with more oil, add a couple of cloves of garlic, the seeds from the vanilla pod and cover with aluminium foil before placing in the oven for 40 minutes at around 180°C.

To plate up, place three discs of potato on the plate then add two or three medallions of the beef and spoon over the sauce. Garnish with fresh thyme.

TRADITIONAL SPANISH TORTILLA

Eggs really are one of nature's superfoods being a perfect protein source and containing almost every vitamin and mineral that our bodies require. They are rich in selenium, a powerful anti-inflammatory, they boost eye health, keep you feeling fuller for longer and so can aid weight loss, are a wonderful source of vitamin D as well as proving an energy boost due to their B vitamin content. Potatoes are low in fat; their resistant starch may boost digestive health and keep you feeling full. Olive oil is a super heart healthy fat. This dish has a three star health rating but beware of the calorie content of the oil.

INGREDIENTS TO SERVE FOUR
AS A STARTER
Cooking 45 minutes

2 large potatoes
5 eggs
Olive oil

Peel the potatoes and slice fairly thinly.

Heat a generous amount of olive oil in a medium frying pan – probably about one and a half inches deep. When hot, add the sliced potatoes. Leave to cook in the pan for around 15-20 minutes until soft and golden.

Halfway through the cooking process once the potatoes have begun to soften, start to break them up a little in the pan with a spatula and continue with this process every five minutes until fully cooked and broken into pieces.

Beat the eggs in a bowl. Remove the potatoes from the heat and with a spatula take sections of the potatoes and press them against the side of the pan to squeeze out some of the excess olive oil before adding to the egg mixture. Repeat this process until all the potatoes have been added to the egg mixture and then stir the mixture well until all the potatoes are incorporated into the eggs.

Heat a little oil in a clean medium frying pan and when hot, add the egg mixture to the pan. After a couple of minutes, once the mixture has set, place a plate over the pan and flip the tortilla onto the plate before sliding back into the pan to cook on the opposite side.

Leave to cook for a couple of minutes more before repeating this process one more time. Allow to cook for a couple more minutes until cooked through then serve either alone or with a crisp green salad.

MEATBALLS IN A CURRY SAUCE

The beef and pork provide protein and the cinnamon and nutmeg provide pain and indigestion relief, boost brain function and aid the liver and kidneys in removing toxins. Cinnamon is excellent at balancing blood sugar levels. The apples provide added fibre and an energy boost whilst curry powder has a huge range of health benefits from cancer and heart disease prevention to a reduction in Alzheimer's and arthritis symptoms. However, given the fat content of the meat, the added wine and the frying of the meatballs, this dish has a one star health rating.

INGREDIENTS FOR SEVEN TO EIGHT PORTIONS

Cooking 1 hour 30 minutes

Please note that the meatballs need to be refrigerated for one hour prior to cooking

———

1kg meat – a mixture of beef and pork

1 egg

1 teaspoon of cinnamon

1 teaspoon of nutmeg

Salt to season

Handful of parsley chopped

For the sauce

2 apples chopped finely

2 onions chopped finely

2 tablespoons of curry powder

Olive oil

1 ltr of white wine

500ml of water

To make the meatballs simply mix all the ingredients together then place in the fridge for a minimum of one hour. Remove from the fridge and using your hands take large teaspoons of the mixture at a time and roll into a ball, roll into some plain flour then set aside.

Once all the mixture has been made into balls, heat a couple of tablespoons of oil in a large pan and add the meatballs. Cook over a medium heat stirring occasionally for around ten minutes until golden on all sides. At this stage they do not need to be cooked through.

Remove the meatballs from the pan and set aside. Heat a little more oil in the same pan, then add the onions and apples and sauté for around ten minutes until the onions are transparent and softened. Add the curry powder, stir well and cook for one minute more. Add the wine and the water and bring to the boil.

Once at boiling point, return the meatballs to the pan and reduce the heat, cover and simmer for around 30 minutes until the sauce has thickened and all is cooked well.

Serve with fresh crusty bread, rice or quinoa.

COFFEE CHEESECAKE

Unfortunately, this dessert is high in fat, sugar and calories and so has a TREAT rating.

INGREDIENTS FOR TWELVE
PORTIONS
Cooking 30 minutes
Please not that this dessert requires refrigerating for a minumum of one hour prior to serving and can be made in advance and stored for upto two days

———

500g cream cheese such as Philadelphia

400g whipping cream

100g sugar

1 sachet cuajada (traditional to Spain only but available on the internet or can be replaced by agar agar or gelatine)

500ml whole milk

Bottle of ready-made Caramel sauce

Digestive biscuits – one to top each cheesecake

Coffee powder for sprinkling

Place the cheese, sugar and cream in a pan and heat on medium until all the ingredients have melted and combined well – around ten/fifteen minutes.

Add the sachet of cuajada to the milk and mix well before adding to the pan. Mix well and increase the heat until the mixture reaches boiling point. Remove from the heat. Take eight individual pots/moulds and pour caramel sauce into the base and a little round the edges of each one. Pour the cheesecake mixture into each mould leaving at least 1cm at the top. Place a digestive biscuit on the top of the mixture in each mould, then sprinkle with a little coffee powder.

Leave to cool at room temperature before placing in the fridge for a minimum of one hour. When ready to serve, remove from the fridge, run a clean small knife around the edge of the mould to loosen before flipping the mould onto a plate.

Sprinkle the plate and cheesecake with a little more coffee powder and serve.

RAUSELL

Rausell Calle Angel Guimera, 61, Valencia

R
ausell is another family-run Spanish restaurant in the heart of the city of Valencia, currently owned by two brothers who are the third generation in their family to run this wonderful establishment. Gorgeous fresh seafood fills the counter displays alongside freshly roasted and salted nuts and cured meats.

I arrived to start my work with them at 4pm, which is usually the end of the lunchtime serving in Spain when the restaurants close until the evening session; however this was not the case at Rausell. There was not one free table and the restaurant was so lively you could have easily mistaken it for a Saturday evening sitting. Fantastic ambience and aroma! Entering their kitchens was a complete delight – and they are huge – which is no surprise given that they have 23 staff running in and out, cooking and serving the most delicious fresh traditional Spanish dishes. And we really did make the most fabulous and delicious food which I highly recommend you try at home. The dishes may look elaborate but believe me they really are quite simple and easy to do – you can create restaurant standard food in no time at all. And if you do ever have the pleasure of eating at Rausell, make sure you visit their deli next door which has a wide range of their freshly cooked food daily to take away.

RED KING PRAWNS

The prawns are an excellent source of protein and provide 9 amino acids – in fact they provide almost the same amount of protein as beef. They are low in fat and calories as well as being an excellent source of omega 3 fatty acids boosting brain and heart health. This dish has a three star health rating.

INGREDIENTS FOR FOUR
PEOPLE AS A STARTER
Cooking 4 minutes

~~~

12 large red King prawns
salt

Simply place the prawns onto a hot grill, season with salt.

After a couple of minutes turn to cook on the other side.

Serve!

PATATAS BRAVAS

The ingredients in this dish are nutritionally sound with the superfood garlic, the heart healthy olive oil and the vitamin, mineral and antioxidant loaded paprika. However, the potatoes are fried to give them that crisp and golden exterior and served with sour cream so as a result they have a one star health rating.

INGREDIENTS FOR SIX TO
EIGHT PEOPLE
Cooking 25 minutes
Thiis is generally served
alongside another main meal or
starter in the form of tapas

———

1kg of potatoes

Paprika

Olive oil

Garlic, minced – the quantity
depends on your personal
preference

Sour cream to serve.

Peel and cut the potatoes into large pieces. Add a large amount of oil to a frying pan and add the potatoes when the oil is hot. Cook the potatoes without the oil exceeding 110 degrees. Once the potatoes are tender, turn up the heat to brown the potatoes and crisp the outside.

Drain the potatoes.

Add the paprika to the olive oil and garlic and mix well and coat all the potatoes.

Serve with sour cream.

CALDERETA DE LANGOSTA: TRADITIONAL SPANISH LOBSTER, CLAMS AND POTATOES

Lobster contains no carbohydrates, hardly any fat, is low in calories yet rich in protein. It is a good source of selenium, zinc, calcium, copper, iron and vitamin A. It is both a heart and brain boosting food, reduces inflammation in the body and boosts energy. Clams are rich in B vitamins which are wonderful for the nervous system, rich in iron and so help to treat and prevent anaemia and an excellent source of selenium thus reducing arthritis symptoms and boosting joint health. The tomato, garlic and onion provide a wonderful immune system boost too. A three star health rating. (Beware of the mercury content of lobster if consuming regularly)

INGREDIENTS TO SERVE TWO PEOPLE
Cooking 20 minutes

2 lobster of between 400–500g

2 medium potatoes boiled and sliced thickly

4 large prawns

8 clams

750ml of fish stock

2 tablespoons of pureed tomatoes (made with tomato, garlic and onion)

1 tablespoon of coffee (the liquid, not the granules)

120ml brandy

Break the lobsters in half and brown on both sides in a large pan with olive oil, then reserve.

Using the same pan that the lobsters were browned in, add the sliced potatoes to reheat. Once these are golden, add the pureed tomato and the brandy and leave for around two minutes to evaporate.

Add the fish stock and then bring to the boil and simmer for five minutes until it reduces a little before adding the lobster back into the pan.

After three minutes, add the clams and prawns. After around two minutes more the clams will open and it will be ready to serve.

ALMOND TART

Eggs are a perfect protein source and contain almost every vitamin and mineral that our bodies require. They are rich in selenium which is a powerful anti-inflammatory, they boost eye health, keep you feeling fuller for longer and so can aid weight loss, are a wonderful source of vitamin D as well as proving an energy boost due to their B vitamin content whilst almonds are rich in antioxidants thus protecting the body from harmful free radicals, diseases and premature ageing. They are rich in vitamin E and magnesium and have been shown to be effective in lowering both blood pressure and cholesterol. This dessert does contain added sugar but still manages a one star health rating.

INGREDIENTS FOR
FOUR PEOPLE
Cooking 1 hour
Please note that this dessert requires cooling and chilling once cooked and prior to serving, so allow sufficient time for this

1 ltr of milk

8 eggs

14 Maria cookies, crushed (these are specific Spanish cookies but you may use rich tea or digestive biscuits)

300g Sugar
250g ground almonds

Place all the ingredients into a bowl and mix well preferably with an electric mixer.

Place into a baking tin and place into a pre heated oven of 165°C for 45 minutes. Remove from the oven, allow to cool, then chill.

Remove from the baking tin, slice and serve with fresh berries and a little cream if desired.

LA PRINCIPAL

Restaurante La Principal, Carrer de Polo y Peyrolon, 5, 46021, Valencia, Spain

This was the very first restaurant that I had the pleasure of visiting when I arrived in Valencia and I have returned many times since. Situated close to the Mestalla Stadium – the home of Valencia Football Club and a firm favourite with its players and staff, it is owned by Rafael Honrubia whose journey in the restaurant business has lasted more than forty years and it is easy to see why. His is a family of restauranteurs whose attention to detail is second to none.

Ingredients are purchased daily early in the morning from the local market and the head chef, Yosue Urgel Gonzalez, then transforms these delicious, fresh, nutritious, locally produced foods into culinary masterpieces. La Principal is a traditional Spanish yet modern restaurant whose tables are full every single day at both sittings for lunch and for dinner – there is also a bar area where smaller and lighter dishes can be ordered. A team of 18 full time staff cater to the every need and request of their loyal customers – I felt extremely privileged to be a part of their amazing team if only for one day!

COD PROFITEROLES

Cod is a low calorie source of protein, rich in heart healthy omega 3 fatty acids as well as Vitamins B12 and B6 and pine nuts can boost energy, aid heart health, curb the appetite and so aid weight loss, strengthen bones and boost the immune system. Parsley really is a super food bursting with vitamin K and an excellent source of vitamin C. It has been proven to reduce the symptoms of or treat inflammation, bad breath, kidney stones, arthritis, bloating and constipation amongst other ailments. Given that these profiteroles are fried they have a one star health rating.

INGREDIENTS PER PERSON
Cooking 40 minutes

Please note that this recipe refers to already cooked fish and potatoes, so please allow time to prepare these in advance. Time also needs to be allowed for chilling prior to cooking

———

250g cod cooked
170g potatoes cooked
40g garlic - fried
40g pine nuts toasted
20g chopped parsley
Tempura – made as follows:
200g flour
400ml water
20g yeast
20g salt
20g sugar

Blend the cod and the garlic and reserve. Mash the potatoes then add the cod and garlic and mix well. Add the pine nuts and parsley, roll into balls and place in the fridge and leave until chilled.

Heat some oil to 200ºC.

Make the tempura and leave to stand for half an hour.

Remove the cod profiteroles from the fridge, coat in the tempura and fry until golden and crispy. Delicious served with aioli.

COD PIL PIL

The cod is a wonderful low calorie source of protein providing heart healthy omega 3 fats and the garlic and peppers reduce blood pressure and cholesterol, boost immune function, detoxify the body, provide fibre and vitamins C and E in abundance. Given the quantity of oil used, this dish has a two star health rating.

INGREDIENTS PER PERSON
Cooking 40 minutes

~~~

220g cod
500ml olive oil
2 garlic cloves
3 small green peppers

Place the cod fillet whole into the olive oil in a pan with one garlic clove sliced. Heat the oil until it reaches 65°C. Once cooked through, remove the cod fillet and set aside. Slice the other clove of garlic and fry in the oil until crispy, remove and set aside. Next fry the peppers and set aside.

Keeping the oil heated to 70°C – with a whisk, continue stirring the olive oil until it thickens and changes to a dense, creamy colour and texture. Once this consistency is reached, remove from the heat and start to plate up.

First place the cod on a plate, pour over the Pil Pil (olive oil sauce), place the three peppers on the top and then finish with the fried garlic slices.

FIDEUA

Calamari is rich in vitamins and minerals in particular B vitamins but it also contains saturated fat, sodium and cholesterol. Prawns are an excellent source of protein and provide 9 amino acids – in fact they provide almost the same amount of protein as beef. They are low in fat and calories as well as being an excellent source of omega 3 fatty acids, boosting brain and heart health whilst lobster is a good source of selenium, zinc, calcium, copper, iron and vitamin A. It is both a heart and brain boosting food, reduces inflammation in the body and boosts energy. This dish has a two star health rating.

INGREDIENTS FOR
TWO PEOPLE
Cooking 30 minutes

—∿∿—

20ml olive oil
80g calamari chopped
6 large red prawns peeled
1 small lobster halved
25g tomato paste
10g paprika
1g saffron
250g fideua
500ml fish stock

Heat the oil in a pan, preferably a paella pan, then add the calamari, lobster and prawns.

Cook a few minutes, then remove the prawns and lobster from the pan (once cooked through) and reserve before adding the tomato, paprika and fideua.

Saute for approximately 4/5 minutes then add the fish stock and the saffron. Saute for between 12/15 minutes until the fideua has absorbed all the stock. Add the prawns and lobster back into the pan. This can be served immediately or as they do in La Principal – place the pan into the oven for a few minutes.

CARAMEL FLAN

Delicious but I am afraid not particularly nutritious and therefore this dessert has a TREAT rating.

55ml water

165g sugar

8 egg yolks

Caramel Sauce

In a pan, mix the water and sugar and heat to 110°C. Remove from the heat and chill for five minutes before adding the egg yolks which have been beaten well. Mix again with a whisk really quickly and strongly. In small flan moulds, pour a layer of caramel (this can be shop bought or homemade) then top with the foamy mixture. Place the moulds into a steam oven at 98°C for approximately 20 minutes until set. Remove and allow to cool before refrigerating.

Serve with chocolate decorations and fresh raspberries.

ASADA AURORA

Asador Aurora, Carrer del Batxiller, 1, 46010, Valencia

This really is a true hidden gem of real Spanish cooking hidden behind the huge ornate wooden doors at the entrance. Recipes that have been passed down through generations, bursting with flavours, each dish consisting of very few ingredients and incredibly simple to make. Asada Aurora has been serving regular clients and tourists for over thirty years averaging fifty places per day and serving their most popular meat dishes of baby lamb and beef from Salamanca. Their open brick oven is impressive and produces flavours that words simply cannot do justice. If you enjoy meat then this is absolutely worth a visit.

KIDNEY BEANS WITH PORK

Kidney beans are bursting with fibre and nutrients, balance blood sugar, combat diabetes and can even aid weight loss. The carrots, onions and garlic in this dish provide a super health boost but the meats, whilst adding extra protein also add fat, resulting in two star health rating for this dish.

INGREDIENTS FOR
FOUR PEOPLE
Cooking 2 hours 30 minutes
Please note that the kidney beans
must be soaked overnight prior to
cooking

—∿∿—

1kg of kidney beans
2 onions chopped
Half a peeled carrot chopped
Half a sweet chorizo sliced
Bone of a ham joint
1 bay leaf
150g Pork snout cut into pieces
10g paprika
1 garlic clove

Soak the kidney beans overnight prior to cooking. Place into a large pan with five litres of water the kidney beans, chorizo, one onion, the garlic clove, the ham bone, the pork, the bay leaf and the carrot. Bring to the boil before lowering the heat and simmering for 2-2.5 hours.

Fry in a little olive oil the second onion with the paprika and add to the pan when there is one hour remaining of the cooking time.

Serve with warm chunky bread.

ROASTED BABY LAMB

Lamb is a healthy source of protein proving a wide range of minerals including calcium, magnesium, selenium, zinc and iron as well as B vitamins. Eating lamb can improve muscle mass, bone health, boost the immune system and promote a healthy nervous system. It is also an excellent source of folic acid which is vital for pregnant women as it prevents birth defects in babies. However, it is also quite high in saturated fat which with over consumption can cause raised cholesterol levels, high blood pressure and kidney stones. Two star health rating.

INGREDIENTS FOR
FOUR PEOPLE
Cooking 2 hours 30 minutes

2 legs of lamb each weighing
approximately 1kg
Water
Salt

Season both legs of lamb on both sides. Place skin down into a pan and add 100ml of water.

Place into an oven heated to 180°C for two hours.

After two hours, turn the legs over and cook for a further 20 minutes.

If during the cooking process the water has evaporated then add more.

The Spanish serve this alone or with bread but it works wonderfully with roasted vegetables also.

ROASTED PIGLET

Oregano is a wonderful herb that boosts the immune system, detoxifies the body, promotes heart health, strengthens the bones and can even boost energy levels and garlic is a wonderful superfood also boosting the immune system and promoting heart health. Piglet is an excellent protein source containing all essential amino acids as well as many vitamins and minerals but it does also contain a significant amount of fat. This dish has a one star health rating.

INGREDIENTS TO SERVE FOUR TO SIX PEOPLE
Cooking 4 hours

Please note that the meat needs to tenderize once marinated for 12 hours prior to cooking.

Half a piglet of around 2.7kg and less than one month old

2 garlic cloves

5g oregano

Salt

15g pig fat/lard

120ml white wine

Water

Crush the garlic with the oregano and salt. Add to the pig fat and the white wine and mix well. Using your hands, rub this mixture over the piglet concentrating on the internal side, then leave for a minimum of 12 hours to marinate and tenderize.

Place the piglet skin down into a pan and add a couple of inches of water.

Cook in an oven heated to 180°C for three hours. Remove from the pan then flambe the skin side with brandy before returning to the oven for a further 30 minutes until the skin becomes extremely crispy.

MARINATED TUNA

Tuna is rich in omega 3 fatty acids which have been proven to aid healthy cholesterol levels. It is also an excellent source of potassium which has been shown to reduce blood pressure, so it really is a super heart healthy food. It is low in fat yet rich in protein and immune boosting nutrients. This is a three star health rated dish.

Tuna steak of approximately 1.5kg weight or 4cm thick

500ml of red wine vinegar

400ml of Extra Virgin Olive oil

250ml of white wine

1g thyme

2g of whole black peppercorns

8 bay leaves

2 garlic cloves halved

Place all the ingredients into a pan, add enough water to cover and boil for 45 minutes. Plate and serve with a little of the juice and olives.

RABO DE TORO
TAIL OF THE BULL

Snails are surprisingly nutritious, providing protein yet little carbohydrates. They are an excellent source of iron (containing more than beef) as well as magnesium and potassium. This dish is also loaded with wonderful vegetables, garlic and spices. Beef is rich in protein and iron as well as being a good source of zinc and B vitamins thus promoting a healthy nervous system and immune system. A two star health rating.

INGREDIENTS FOR FOUR PEOPLE
Cooking 4 hours 30 minutes

2kg beef cut into large pieces
4 dozen snails (optional)
2 onions diced
3 carrots
1 whole head of garlic
1 stick of celery
2 leeks
2 bay leaves
Salt and pepper to season
A pinch of cinnamon
A pinch of ground clove
Olive oil
240ml of sweet port wine
240ml of brandy
Water

Brown the beef in the olive oil, season with salt and pepper before adding the vegetables (chopped fairly thickly) and stir well.

Add the sweet wine and brandy and flambe for a minute or two. Leave on a medium heat until the liquid has reduced by half before adding some water just to cover the ingredients in the pan.

Add the spices, cover and leave to cook on a medium heat for three to four hours depending on the cut and thickness of the meat chosen. Remove the meat from the pan and set aside, then blend the vegetables and the liquid until smooth.

Add both back to the pan and bring back to the boil.

If using the snails (pre-cook these in advance) add in at this point.

Season with salt and pepper and serve.
(If the liquid is too watery and clear then add a little cornstarch and leave to thicken a little longer)

LA OLLA DE CALABAZA
PAN OF PUMPKIN

Pumpkin is bursting with fibre and so promotes healthy intestines as well as keeping you fuller for longer. Rich in vitamin A which is wonderful for both eye and skin health. Rich in tryptophan- the amino acid that helps the body make serotonin and thus promotes relaxation and improved sleep. White beans or cannellini beans are rich in protein and fibre and protect the body from harmful toxins. They are a good source of iron, antioxidants and vitamin K. They are a heart health, bone health, intestine, brain health and energy boosting food. Celery is rich in minerals such as magnesium, calcium, copper, iron and zinc as well as many vitamins. It boosts heart health, detoxifies the body and may even protect against urinary tract infections. It helps to balance fluid in the body and is also good for reducing the symptoms of arthritis and gout as it is a wonderful natural anti inflammatory. This dish does have a little added sugar but still receives a three star health rating.

INGREDIENTS FOR
FOUR PEOPLE
Cooking 2 hours 15 minutes
Pleae note that the beans must be soaked overnight prior to cooking

—ᴡᴡ—

5ltr of water

200g celery peeled and chopped

600g of pumpkin, peeled and chopped

400g potatoes peeled and cut into chunks

200g white beans soaked in water overnight

2 tablespoons of sugar

A little saffron

Salt

Place all the ingredients into a large pan and once it reaches boiling point add the following mixture: Place into a frying pan one tablespoon of olive oil, 4 cloves of garlic chopped, 150g diced onion. Once the onion becomes transparent, add a tablespoon of paprika, one sliced ripe tomato and cook over a medium heat.

Add this mixture to the pumpkin mixture and leave to cook for around one and a half hours until the beans are soft.

Add 300g of rice and cook for a further 15-17 minutes stirring continually until the rice is soft. Season with salt and serve.

This dish can be served hot or cold.

SPANISH TART

Despite the egg and Greek yoghurt content of this dish, I am afraid it still only has a TREAT health rating.

INGREDIENTS FOR 12 PEOPLE
Cooking 1 hour 30 minutes
Please note that once cooked this dessert must be chilled to set prior to serving

—◊—

For the cake base:
250g sugar
375g all purpose flour
3 eggs
2 teaspoons of vanilla extract
1 tablespoon of baking powder
125ml sunflower Oil
125g plain Greek yoghurt

For the top of the tart:
3 sachets of cuajada
(as before this is a common product here in Spain but less so in the UK but it can be purchased online)

10 tablespoons sugar
1.5ltr milk
300ml cream

Preheat the oven to 200ºC.

Separate the eggs and add the yolks to the yoghurt and place the whites in a separate bowl and whisk until they form soft peaks.

Add the oil and the sugar to the yoghurt and yolks and mix well then add the vanilla essence. Stir in the egg whites.

Sieve the baking powder and flour into the mixture and mix well.

Pour the mixture into a rectangle cake tin that has been greased and floured then place in the oven. Reduce the heat to 180ºC and cook for around 50 minutes.

The cake is done when a knife inserted into the centre comes out clean.

Remove from the oven and leave in the tray to cool.

Place one litre of milk and the sugar into a pan and bring to the boil. Once it starts to boil add the cream and stir. Mix the sachets of cuajada with the remaining milk, then add into the warm milk stirring continuously. Continue stirring for approximately four minutes, then remove from the heat.

Pour the mixture over the cooled cake in the baking tray then place in the fridge to set.

Once set, tip the baking tray upside down onto a serving tray.

ALQUERIA DEL POU

Alqueria del Pou. Entrado Rico, 6, Valencia, Spain

isiting and working alongside head chef Toni Gomez in Restaurante Del Pou was an incredible experience. Set amongst their own crop yielding fields, this beautiful traditional Spanish farm looking restaurant is full to capacity every single day serving over 200 people for lunch on a daily basis and I quickly found out why. The HUGE team of chefs start early each morning carefully preparing the fresh produce either from their own fields which on the day I visited were full of onions ready to be picked, or from local suppliers.

The restaurant is situated just minutes from the sea front and the fish and seafood is always a popular choice. Toni is both passionate and charismatic and his dishes maintain the traditional Spanish feel and culture whilst at the same time capturing his vision and flare for the 'out of the ordinary'. Ordinary his food most certainly is not. Coming from a whole family of chefs, Toni was extremely proud to tell me how Alqueria Del Pou is the current title holder of the best Paella which despite being a Spanish dish is actually a worldwide competition – so they are the world title holders. The customers at this restaurant range from the regular locals, to tourists, to gastronomy enthusiasts to the larger commercial events and weddings. I cannot wait to share with you the wonderful food that we cooked and that you will easily be able to recreate in your own kitchen.

ENSALADA VALENCIANA

This dish is a powerhouse of nutrients, essential fats boosting heart and brain health, fibre keeping the intestines healthy and rich in a wide range of vitamins and minerals. A three star health rating.

INGREDIENTS QUANTITIES TO
SUIT NUMBERS
Preparation 5 minutes

⁓

Lettuce

Sliced onion

Tomato

Olives

Tuna in olive oil

1 Hot pepper

Dried Tuna (optional as less common in England than in Spain)

Cooked asparagus

Anchovy

Salt

Olive oil

Vinegar

Quite simply wash the lettuce, tomato and pepper and slice the onion and tomato. Place the lettuce in the base of a bowl and build the salad on top, topping with the tuna and anchovy. Season with a little salt and drizzle with olive oil and vinegar.

OCTOPUS WITH SALSA ROMESCU AND PAPRIKA OIL

This dish has so many wonderful ingredients, the low calorie yet high in protein octopus bursting with iron and B vitamins so preventing anaemia and boosting both the nervous system and immune system. The niacin content also assists the body in turning protein, carbohydrates and fats into energy. The garlic is a wonderful immune boosting, heart healthy, cancer preventative and blood pressure lowering addition whilst the paprika adds a wonderful boost of antioxidants protecting the body from illnesses and anti-ageing as well and being highly antibacterial. The cream does add fat and calories to this dish resulting in a two star health rating.

INGREDIENTS FOR TWO PEOPLE
Cooking 15 minutes
(not including the salsa)

Please note that the salsa is best prepared in advance and also this recipe uses potatoes already cooked *al dente* so allow time to prepare these in advance

(PER PERSON)
700g octopus cooked
250ml cream
3 new potatoes cooked *al dente*
Handful parsley chopped
2 onions sliced
2 tomatoes halved
5 cloves of garlic
Handful of raw almonds
25ml white wine vinegar
Olive oil, Paprika, Salt, Pepper

To prepare the salsa romescu:
Roast in the oven the sliced onions, halved tomatoes, four garlic cloves and the handful of raw almonds for 40 minutes at 200°. Once cooked, remove from the oven and blend with 100ml of olive oil, 25ml of white wine vinegar and season with salt and pepper. Set aside.

Chop the parsley and then place in a pan and saute with the remaining clove of garlic crushed. Add the cream and a pinch of salt before cooking over a medium heat for 6 or 7 minutes. Add the cooked potatoes to the pan until heated through.

Meanwhile, place the precooked octopus into a pan over a high heat and cook for a few minutes on both sides until golden.

Remove the potatoes from the parsley cream and place onto a plate spooning over a little more of the cream once plated. Balance the octopus on top of the potatoes.

Drizzle with the salsa Romescu before topping with a little paprika oil and a pinch of rock/sea salt.

SEAFOOD CASSEROLE

The fish in this dish is a wonderfully healthy source of protein as well as containing selenium, phosphorus, magnesium and zinc boosting bone health and of course those wonderful omega 3 fatty acids aiding a healthy heart, brain and the joints too. The tomatoes provide a boost of vitamins A, C and K as well as anti oxidants, boost both eye and heart health, aid digestion, promote healthy skin and can even prevent gallstones. However, the fish is fried in this dish (albeit in olive oil) therefore it has a two star health rating.

INGREDIENTS TO SERVE TWO PEOPLE
Cooking 25 minutes

For the fish, you can choose whatever type you wish as long as it is skinned, filleted and deboned.

We used sword fish, Red Sea scorpion fish and john dory – one small fillet of each

4 whole giant prawns

4 langoustines

10 clams in shells

Flour for coating

2 cloves of garlic chopped

Tinned chopped tomato

Olive oil

Salt

Fish stock

Coat the fish fillets on both sides with flour and fry in a little olive oil for a few minutes on each side until cooked, then remove and set aside. In a large frying pan add 50ml of olive oil, then add the langoustines and prawns, season with salt – cook for a few minutes, then set aside.

In the same pan, add the chopped garlic and four dessert spoons of chopped tomatoes and saute for a few minutes until cooked through before adding 200ml of fish stock.

Once heated, add the cooked fish filets, the cooked seafood and the clams. Cook over a medium heat for around 6 or 7 minutes until the stock has reduced.

Plate up the fish and seafood and pour over the fish stock.

ARNADI

This does not actually have a translation into English so to best describe it would be a delicious pumpkin and sweet potato tart. Rarely does a dessert receive a three star health rating but this one most certainly does.

Ingredients for 15 portions
Cooking 6 hours 30 minutes

―⁓―

1 medium pumpkin

2 sweet potatoes

6 eggs

Half a tablespoon of ground cinnamon

Ground almonds

Lemon zest

Peel the pumpkin and the sweet potatoes, remove the seeds from the pumpkin, then roast them in the oven until the flesh is completely soft.

Mash the two roasted vegetables together until smooth.

Add the eggs, the lemon zest and the cinnamon and mix well. Grease muffin trays or pre bought foil individual moulds with butter then fill each one to almost full with the mixture.

Top with the ground almonds.

Place in the oven for 5 hours at 100°C.

Remove from the oven. Top with a little chopped almond, drizzle with honey and decorate with a slice of lemon or lime.

Can be served either warm or cold.

PAN FRIED CALAMARI

Cslamari is rich in protein therefore sustaining energy and building muscle. It is rich in anti oxidants and vitamin B12 as well as potassium, iron and phosphorous thus boosting the immune system, bone and blood cell health. The garlic and parsley oil makes this dish even more nutritious and therefore it is a three star rated dish.

INGREDIENTS PER PERSON
Coooking 6-8 minutes

—⁓—

1 calamari of 250–300g
Garlic and parsley oil

Keeping the calamari whole, slice it into sections as shown in the image.

Place onto a hot plate or into a hot frying pan with a little olive oil and cook until golden on both sides.

Once cooked, place onto a plate twisting into a circular shape and place any additional pieces decoratively on top.

Generously drizzle with a dressing of olive oil, chopped parsley and crushed garlic.

LUBINA A LA SAL
SALTED SEABASS

Seabass is a low calorie excellent source of protein. It is also a fantastic source of omega 3 and selenium. However, it does contain a significant amount of mercury so should be consumed in moderation by children and pregnant women. That said this remains a three star health rated dish.

INGREDIENTS FOR TWO PEOPLE
Cooking 30 minutes

One whole seabass weighing around 800-900g prepared ready to cook

2kg of sea salt

Preheat the oven to 230 degrees.
Onto a baking tray place a layer of salt, then place the whole seabass on top.

Cover the whole of the seabass with a generous coating of salt then place into the hot oven for around 22 minutes.

Remove from the oven, remove the salt, peel the skin back and plate one half of the fish on each plate, removing any bones in the process.

Serve with roasted or sautéed vegetables.

(To serve this in the restaurant as they bring the dish to the table before removing the crusted salt, they pour a small amount of alcohol onto the salt and light it. It looks incredibly impressive, smells wonderful and is most entertaining. The flames die down naturally after a minute or so)

STRAWBERRIES AND CREAM

Strawberries are a powerful antioxidant and do not rapidly raise blood sugar making them a good choice for diabetics. Their polyphenol content has a preventative effect against heart disease. They are also rich in fibre and potassium and a natural anti inflammatory. However the cream and sugar in this dish result in it being a one star health rated dessert.

INGREDIENTS PER PERSON
Cooking 5 minutes

———〜〜〜———

100-200g mini strawberries
(these must be really fresh, no
more than a couple of days old)

250 ml cream

150g sugar

Whip the cream and sugar until stiff enough to pipe.

Place half of the strawberries into the bottom of a glass serving dish.

Pipe the cream into the dish, then top decoratively with the remaining strawberries.

Decorate the plate and serve.

RESTAURANTE GABRINUS

Restaurante Gabrinus, Avenida Del Cerro, Numero 15, 46392, Valencia

It was a real treat for me to have the opportunity to visit Restaurante Gabrinus and cook with one of the owners and head chef, Teresa Carrascosa Sanchez. She and her husband Salvador opened Gabrinus in 1999, after previously owning a tapas bar in their home town. However, this was quite a transformation. Situated in the middle of farmland and high above the city Gambrinus specialises in hearty dishes and they cook everything from scratch on the premises whether that be the mayonnaise or the bread.

All the ingredients are bought from the famous Mercado de Valencia which stocks the finest fresh and natural produce and their menu caters for all, serving everything from meatballs, snails and octopus to rices, stews and lots and lots of meat. The dishes that Teresa and Salvador were kind enough to share with me are definitely unique but true Spanish cooking that has been passed down generations. I hope that you enjoy them as much as I did.

LENTEJAS DE LA BAÑEZA
A DELIGHTFUL HEARTY LENTIL DISH

Lentils are mighty in terms of nutritional benefits, rich in cholesterol lowering and healthy intestine promoting fibre. They are an excellent source of iron, rich in folate and magnesium boosting heart health and aiding muscle relaxation and they have an amazing ability to balance blood sugar levels. The carrots are rich in fibre, beta carotene and antioxidants. A super eye health boosting food, their potassium content aids the regulation of blood pressure and their vitamin C content and anti-bacterial qualities make them a super immune boosting food too. Add the garlic, paprika and onion and this is a powerhouse of nutrients. The ham is a good source of protein, however it may add fat and sodium, therefore this dish receives a two star health rating.

INGREDIENTS FOR SIX PEOPLE
Cooking 4 hours 45 minutes

1.5kg lentils
500g carrots, chopped
200g red pepper, chopped
400g onion, chopped
10g sweet paprika
150ml olive oil
200g fresh tomato, chopped
4 bay leaves
1 whole garlic
1kg of ham on the bone sliced into thick slices (including the bone) (ask your butcher to pre slice this for you)
1kg of piglets' feet
800g of pigs' ears and snout, chopped

Place 3 litres of water into a large pan and add the ham bone pieces and whole garlic. Bring to the boil and simmer for around one hour. Remove the fat from the surface of the water.

In a frying pan with a little olive oil, lightly fry the piglet feet, ears and snout pieces for around 15 minutes then add to the pan of water and continue simmering.

In the same frying pan, add the carrots, peppers, onions, tomatoes and paprika and saute for around 10 minutes, then set aside.

Two hours after adding the piglet feet and ears and snout to the pan add the lentils to the simmering water. Fifteen minutes later add the sautéed vegetable mixture. Continue simmering until the lentils are cooked through – probably 30 minutes more.

Serve with freshly baked bread or a fresh side salad.

AJO-RRIERO
A LIGHT GARLIC POTATO AND COD PUREE

Potatoes provide good levels of vitamin C, potassium, B vitamins calcium and fibre whilst the cod is a wonderful lean source of protein, rich in omega 3 fatty acids. Garlic provides an additional boost to both the heart and immune system and the egg yolks boost vitamin D levels - all in all this really is a three star health rated dish.

INGREDIENTS FOR SIX PEOPLE
Cooking 50 minutes

—ww—

1kg potatoes in their skins
500g cod (cooked and flaked)
1ltr extra virgin olive oil
1 whole garlic bulb, crushed
2 egg yolks

Boil the potatoes until soft, remove from the pan and peel. (I was advised not to peel the potatoes before cooking as the water penetrates the potato and leaves it too mushy and not the correct consistency for this particular dish).

Once peeled, mash the potatoes then add to a mixer. Add the garlic and turn the mixer on slow. Slowly add the olive oil little by little, continuing mixing at all times. If the mixture becomes runny before incorporating all the olive oil then do not add the total amount. The exact amount required depends of the type of potatoes used and the end consistency should be light and fluffy but with a mash- like appearance.

Add the cooked cod and continue mixing until smooth. Finally add the two egg yolks and mix until fully incorporated.

When finished it should have a light spongy mousse-like texture.

Pour onto plates and garnish with a little fresh parsley. Serve with freshly baked bread.

For the syrup:

200g sugar

250ml water

For the meringue:

200g sugar

250ml water

8 egg whites

Place the sugar and water in a pan and cook over a high heat for around ten minutes without stirring until a syrup has formed. Add 10ml of dark rum and stir.

Drizzle this syrup over the warm cake and allow to absorb.

Add the sugar and water to the pan and heat over a high heat without stirring until a syrup has formed – until it is almost boiling.

Mix the egg whites until they form soft peaks, then add the syrup mixture whilst continuing to mix. Once fully incorporated, place the meringue mixture into a piping bag and pipe over the whole tart covering both the top and sides.

Place back into the oven for a further ten minutes until the top of the meringue is toasted.

Slice and serve.

OSCAR TORRIJOS

I was extremely honoured to be able to visit the home of the famous Spanish chef Oscar Torrijos and learn some wonderful recipes of famous Spanish dishes. Oscar spent over an hour telling me of his life and journey which led to his incredible success. Oscar wanted to be a mechanic after growing up in a rural area and spending a lot of time with large farm machinery; however, the decision which led him down the culinary route was made by his parents who saw his cousin working hard as a waiter and wanted Oscar to do the same. Contact was made with a local restaurant and a waiter he became – but not for long. His interest in cooking grew so rapidly and so quickly did he learn that before long he had moved into the kitchen and become a kitchen helper and later an apprentice. Oscar then went on to catering college and his studies took him to Switzerland and China and he later studied French cuisine.

He went on to own several restaurants that served not only Spanish foods but cuisine from all over the world. Oscar was keen to bring all that he had learned from his travels back to Spain to enable the Spanish to 'taste a little of the world'. He has written various books including one of rice dishes and another on cheeses before retiring from being full time in the kitchen in 2013 and starting to train other professional chefs. However, despite his retirement, it is clear that Oscar is not finished yet. He is currently pondering over an offer to move abroad again to work for a large restaurant chain and told me that he will never stop learning. I most certainly learned a lot from this inspiring man which I am thrilled to be able to share with you in my book.

GAZPACHO MANCHEGO

This is a hearty traditional farmers' dish as opposed to a light soup that you may be used to seeing. Partridge is an excellent source of protein and lower in both fat and cholesterol than both beef and chicken. It contains good levels of iron and no saturated fatty acids. It also contains the highest levels of selenium of all other meat. Selenium is vital for the reproductive system, heart, psychological and thyroid health. It also boosts the immune system, detoxifies the body and promotes healthy skin and hair. Mushrooms are high in antioxidants and also provide vitamin D whilst the garlic, tomatoes and pepper all provide added nutrients and fibre. This dish has a two star health rating.

INGREDIENTS FOR SIX PEOPLE
Cooking 1 hour 20 minutes

———

Half a rabbit

Half a hare

1 partridge

5 cloves of garlic

Half a green pepper (optional) chopped finely

200g tomato, with skin and seeds removed then chopped

2 bay leaves

1 sprig of rosemary and 1 sprig of thyme

300g mushrooms quartered

100ml of olive oil

1 torto gazpachera cut into small pieces (This can be purchased online) – aim for 80g per person

Cut all the meats into even sized pieces.

Put the oil into a large pan and heat then add the meats and season with salt and pepper. Fry over a medium heat. Once the meat starts to golden add the garlic cloves smashed but with the skin still on.

Add the pepper and tomatoes and allow to cook for a further five minutes before adding the mushrooms and mixing well. Allow all the ingredients to cook for a further five minutes before adding the water to cover. Add the thyme and rosemary.

Simmer for 20-25 minutes removing any fat from the surface throughout.

Once cooked through, remove the meat from the pan and remove all bones before adding the meat only back to the pan together with the chopped torta. Turn off the heat and cover with a lid. Leave to stand for 15 minutes.

With a mortar and pestle, crush one clove of garlic and add the cumin and saffron (toasted) and some

Salt and pepper

1 teaspoon of cumin

4-5 litres of water

A couple of strands of saffron

black pepper. Then using a little of the stock from the pan make a paste.

Add this paste to the large pan, mix well and then heat once again to just below boiling point. Season with salt and pepper if required.

Serve hot.

LAMB WITH BROAD BEANS

Broad beans are rich in both protein and fibre as well as providing a range of vitamins and minerals. They are an excellent source of iron thus preventing anaemia and boosting brain health and their vitamin C content boosts immunity and the production of collagen in the body. Lamb is also an excellent source of protein as well as iron, zinc, selenium and vitamin B12 so boosting energy, memory and brain function and the nervous system too. Leeks belong to the same family as garlic and onions of Allium vegetables and share many of the same health benefits, rich in flavonoids which protect our blood vessels as well as folate. Carrots, onions and tomatoes add beta carotene to boost eye health, fibre, boost both the immune and digestive systems and detoxify the body. A two star health rated dish.

INGREDIENTS FOR SIX-EIGHT PEOPLE

Cooking 2 hours for the first part with the lamb then 1 hour 15 minutes the following day to complete the dish.

Please note that part of this dish requires making in advance and refrigerating overnight and the broad beans must also be soaked in water overnight prior to cooking

⸻

For the lamb:

3 necks of lamb 2.8kg approx. cut in half lengthways

2 onions

3 carrots

Half a leek

3 large tomatoes

In a large pan, brown the lamb that has been seasoned and rubbed with olive oil then remove from the pan and set aside. Using the same pan, add the vegetables chopped thickly and cook for five minutes. Add the fresh herbs, some pepper to season, then add the white wine and heat. Add the lamb to the pan and cook until the wine has reduced by half.

Add enough water to the pan to cover the ingredients, then place in the oven at 190°C. Leave uncovered for the first half an hour and turn the lamb during cooking. Add more water if required, then cover with a lid of baking paper. Continue cooking and turning the lamb occasionally until the meat is cooked and comes away from the bone easily. At this point remove from the oven and allow to stand.

Remove the meat from the pan and place onto a board covered in cling film. Spread the lamb with mustard before sprinkling with pepper and a little chopped rosemary and thyme. Taking the cling

1 whole garlic

50ml sunflower oil

1 bottle of white wine

Sprigs of fresh herbs

Salt and pepper to season

Mustard

For the beans:

1kg of broad beans, soaked in water overnight

2 tomatoes, peeled and chopped into 8mm size pieces

1 onion, peeled and chopped into 8mm size pieces

1 onion, sliced in half

1 bay leaf

2 green peppers, chopped into 8mm size pieces

2 cloves of garlic, crushed

Sprigs of parsley

Olive oil

1 tablespoon of butter

Salt and pepper

film at one end, roll the lamb whilst still hot into rolls and ensure they are formed and compact. Allow to cool a little before refrigerating for 24 hours.

Add the beans, herbs, ground pepper and onion sliced in half to a pan with a splash of olive oil and a bay leaf. Once the pan is hot add enough water just to cover the beans. Simmer until cooked through around 45 minutes. Remove the beans from the pan then set aside.

Using the same pan and stock, add all remaining ingredients and cook for around 20 minutes before adding the beans back to the stock to heat through.

Remove the cling film and slice the rolls of lamb to the thickness you desire, brush with a little butter and heat in an oven until golden.
Serve with the beans, a little of the stock and garnish with thyme, rosemary and parsley.

TORTILLA HORTELENA GUISADA
GARDEN TORTILLA

This dish really is an energy boosting, muscle building, immune system strengthening and detoxifying dish. Aubergines are bursting with fibre and so promote healthy intestines and keep everything regular as well as being an excellent source of magnesium, manganese and B vitamins. This dish does contain a significant amount of olive oil but given the health benefits of this wonderful oil, this dish still retains a three star health rating.

INGREDIENTS FOR
FOUR PEOPLE
Cooking 35-40 minutes

500g peeled potatoes, cut into quarters then sliced to around 3mm thickness

200g onions, cut into quarters then sliced into 2mm thickness

1 aubergine, not peeled, sliced in half lengthways, then each half sliced lengthways into four, then cut into 3mm thickness

100g red pepper, chopped

2 garlic cloves, peeled and sliced

150ml olive oil

6 eggs

Salt

Place the olive oil and garlic into a wide based frying pan and heat. Add the potato slices and mix well then add the onion and pepper and season with salt. Cook over a hot heat stirring occasionally bringing all the ingredients together. After around 15 minutes, add the aubergine and mix well.

Cover the pan. Continue to stir occasionally.

Once the potatoes and all the ingredients are soft, drain them to remove any excess oil.

Beat the eggs and add to the cooked ingredients and mix well before pouring into a large frying pan or tortilla pan preheated with a little olive oil. Stir the mixture over a high heat, then after a few minutes reduce to a medium heat and leave to set and cook. Once the base is golden, place a large plate over the top of the pan to enable you to flip the tortilla over onto the plate, then return to the pan with the golden side facing upwards to enable the other side to cook through.

In Spain, they tend to eat their tortillas slightly runny but this is just personal preference.

This dish can be eaten hot or cold and is also great to eat the next day.

FABADA AUSTRIANA
BEAN AND PORK STEW

Butter beans are a low calorie, protein rich, healthy carbohydrate food rich in protein, fibre, iron and B vitamins. Saffron contains anti-cancer properties, boosts vitality and has been shown to increase memory and concentration, whilst paprika adds a boost of vitamins A and E as well as iron. Black pudding is virtually carb free yet loaded with protein, iron, calcium and magnesium. Pancetta, despite being a meat, is actually low in protein yet high in calories and fats; therefore this dish receives a two star health rating

INGREDIENTS FOR
EIGHT–TEN PEOPLE

Cooking 90 minutes for the stock plus 2 hours 45 minutes for the dish.

Please note that the butter beans must be soaked in water overnight prior to cooking and the stock can be made in advance and stored in the fridge.

———

1kg butter beans, soaked overnight in water

3 black puddings

3 chorizos

300g cured smoked pancetta soaked overnight in hot water

300g shoulder of pork soaked overnight in hot water

1 tablespoon of sweet paprika

10 strands of saffron

100g butter

500ml olive oil

Cook the black pudding and the chorizo for five minutes in boiling water to remove any excess fat then set aside.

In a large pan, place the drained beans then cover with water two cm above the level of the beans.

Add the chorizo, black puddings, pancetta, a splash of olive oil and the butter. Cover and cook over a medium heat for 30 minutes, then turn off the heat.

Add a splash of olive oil to a frying pan and fry the onion for around 5 minutes, then add the paprika being careful not to burn it. Add the bean mixture and the saffron and continue to cook once again removing any fat or impurities that rise to the surface. Take care not to break the beans and to stir gently.

Cook on a low heat for between one and a half and two hours adding chicken stock whenever required.

Once cooked through and soft, turn off the heat and remove the meats from the pan. Cut the pancetta, black pudding and chorizo into large pieces.

100g chopped onion

Salt to season

For the chicken stock:
One chicken carcase with some remaining chicken, one leek, chopped, 2 carrots, chopped, sprigs of herbs, 6 whole black peppercorns, 4ltr of water

Serve the beans onto a plate or bowl and garnish with the meats and black pudding.

Place all the ingredients in a pan and cook for around 90 minutes. Remove any fat or impurities from the top of the water throughout. Strain and you should have around 2 litres of chicken stock.

LECHE MERENGADA WITH FARTONS
SWEET WHIPPED ICE CREAM WITH HOMEMADE ECLAIRS

Apart from the added sugar, this delightful dessert actually has many health benefits. The milk adds calcium and vitamin D as well as some protein boosting both heart and bone health and building and repairing muscles. Lemon zest aids the body in removing toxins, boosts circulation and can reduce cholesterol levels. Cinnamon is rich in antioxidants, a natural anti-inflammatory, protects the brain and even fights infections. The cherries on the top promote sleep due to the melatonin content, regulate blood pressure, reduces the symptoms of arthritis and gout and can prevent muscle soreness post exercise. A one star health rated food.

INGREDIENTS FOR EIGHT PEOPLE

Cooking 45 minutes for the leche plus chilling, 2 hours for the eclairs including rising time. They will also require time to cool prior to icing and serving. 15 minutes cooking time is also required for the cherries for decorating. Please note that part of this recipe requires making in advance and storing in the fridge for a minimum of 12 hours or overnight prior to completing the dish

———

For the leche merengada

1ltr whole milk

The peel of one whole lemon but only the yellow part

Half a cinnamon stick

3 egg whites, beaten until they form stiff peaks

180g sugar

Ground cinnamon to decorate

Place the milk, cinnamon stick, lemon peel and sugar in a pan and bring to the boil. Turn off the heat and allow to cool before refrigerating overnight or for a minimum of 12 hours.

Strain the mixture then place into an ice cream maker.

Half way through the freezing process, add the egg whites, then finish the process.

If serving alone then this looks wonderful served in a glass and sprinkled with the ground cinnamon. However in this case we are going to serve it with our home made eclairs.

Fartons caseros – home made éclairs

INGREDIENTS FOR EIGHT
PIECES APPROXIMATELY

———

200ml water

100g yeast

1200g strong flour

4 eggs

200g sugar

1 teaspoon of salt

Cherries for decorating

500g of fresh ripe sweet cherries

125g sugar

One lemon

For the glaze:

Mix 100g of icing sugar with 2 tablespoons of hot water (when ready to glaze, not in advance).

Sieve the flour into a bowl, then make a well in the centre and add the eggs. Mix with lukewarm water, the yeast the sugar and salt.

Add the oil and mix well to form a dough. Knead the dough and form into a ball shape.

Leave in a warm place for 30 minutes to rise, covered with a tea towel or cling film. It should double in size.

Once risen, cut the dough into pieces the size of your choice, then leave for a further 15 minutes.

Roll into an éclair shape then place onto a baking sheet covered with baking paper. Cover with a tea towel and leave for another 40 minutes in an ambient temperature during which time they will once again double in size.

Cook in a preheated oven at 200ºC for 12-15 minutes. Remove and place on a cooling rack.

Once they have cooled to lukewarm, make the glaze and cover the top of each éclair with the glaze.

Once cooled completely, dust with icing sugar. Keep in an airtight container and consume within two days.

Wash and pit the cherries and place in a pan with the sugar. Grate the zest of half the lemon into the cherries, then squeeze the juice of half the lemon into the pan. Cover and cook until the sugar dissolves for around 4-5 minutes. Uncover and cook for a further 5 minutes stirring occasionally until the cherries are plump and juicy.

To serve our completed dessert, place one glazed eclair on each plate and top with the cooked cherries. Serve with two scoops of the leche merengada. Oscar chose to place his on a thin biscuit base but as you already have the eclair this is not necessary and is personal preference.

RICE PUDDING ROLL WITH APRICOT COMPOTE

BIZCOCHO DE SOLETILLA: A TRADITONAL SPONGE CAKE IN SPAIN AND WILL BE USED AS PART OF THE RICE PUDDING DESSERT

While this dish does have various nutrients derived from the apricots - rich in fibre, Vitamins A, C, K and E and wonderful for treating indigestion and constipation, as well as the eggs and milk adding calcium, protein and vitamin D, it really is high in both sugar and calories and therefore receives a TREAT rating.

INGREDIENTS FOR FOUR-SIX PEOPLE

Cooking 35 minutes for the cake, 45 minutes for the rice pudding, 25 minutes for the apricot compote.

Please not that the rice pudding must be chilled prior to assembling the cake and the apricot compote must be made the day prior and chilled overnight in the fridge.

—⁓—

360g egg whites
220g sugar
200g egg yolk
125g cornflour
125g strong flour

Beat the egg whites until stiff, then add the sugar little by little whilst continue to whisk. Sieve the cornflour and strong flour together into a bowl.

Add the egg yolks to the egg whites and mix gently with a spatula so as not to collapse the egg whites. Add the sieved flours and incorporate with the spatula.

Line a baking tray measuring 60cm x 40cm with baking paper and pour the mixture into the tray. Cook at 200°C for around 10 minutes.

For the creamy rice pudding:

100g pudding rice or uncooked white rice

2ltr whole milk

100g caster sugar

Peel of one orange

1 stick of cinnamon

Freshly ground cinnamon

4 sheets of gelatine

For the apricot compote:

1kg apricots with the stone removed and then halved

300g sugar

1 vanilla pod

5 sheets of gelatine

Cook the rice for four minutes in water, drain and wash. Place the milk in a pan and heat. Once it is warm add the rice and simmer for around 15 minutes. Add the stick of cinnamon and the orange peel then continue to simmer, now stirring continuously until cooked and the rice is soft – around a further 10-15 minutes. The consistency you are looking for is really soft and creamy.

Add the sugar and stir, still on the heat, for a few minutes more. Remove from the heat and leave to cool before refrigerating. (At this point this can be served solely as rice pudding both hot or cold, sprinkled with ground cinnamon.)

For the recipe we are creating here, when the sugar is added with a few minutes left of cooking, add four sheets of gelatine. Prior to serving remove the peel and cinnamon stick.

Place the sugar, the seeds from the vanilla pod and the apricots into a pan with a little water (50ml) and cook until the liquid has evaporated over a low heat. Add the gelatine and mix well.

Remove the mixture and place into cling film and form a roll of around 2cm thickness, then place in the fridge for 24 hours.

Now to assemble:
Place the cake onto a board lined with clingfilm with the lightest part of the cake touching the film. Spread a layer of the apricot jam over the cake followed by a layer of the chilled rice pudding of around 5mm thickness. Take the roll of apricot compote, remove the film and place onto the cake at one side. Then, using the film to assist, roll the cake with the compote in the centre and fasten to hold in shape with the cling film. Place into the fridge for 24 hours before serving and to allow the cake to hold its shape.

TARTA DE SANTIAGA CLASICA
CLASSIC CAKE FROM SANTIAGO (SUPER FAMOUS IN SPAIN)

Almonds are rich in antioxidants and fibre, are well known for reducing cholesterol levels and boosting heart health, wonderful for the skin, boost brain function and control blood sugar levels. The cinnamon also reduces inflammation and boosts immunity. Healthier than a normal cake but remains a TREAT rated dish.

INGREDIENTS TO SERVE
10 PEOPLE
Cooking 45 minutes plus cooling

~~~

6 eggs
300g caster sugar
300g fresh ground almonds
1 zest of one whole lemon
1 tablespoon of freshly ground cinnamon

Icing sugar to decorate
60g melted butter just about to boil (optional)

Mix the ground almonds with the ground cinnamon and lemon zest.

In a bowl place the eggs with the caster sugar and mix delicately so as not to introduce too much air. Add the almonds, cinnamon and lemon zest (and butter if using) and mix until you have a light and well incorporated dough.

Grease a round cake tin of 22cm diameter and line with baking paper then place the mixture into the tin and cook in a preheated oven at 180°C for 30 minutes.

Remove from the oven and leave to cool. Sprinkle with icing sugar and it is ready to serve.

CREMA CATALAN CON HELADO DE CANELA: CATALAN CREAM WITH CINNAMON ICE CREAM

This dish is rich in egg yolks and therefore a wonderful source of vitamin D, B vitamins and vitamins A, E and K, a super bone building food and wonderful for a healthy nervous system. However, it is also high in fat, calories and sugar making it a TREAT rated food.

INGREDIENTS FOR FOUR PEOPLE

Cooking 1 hour for the crema catalan plus 20 minutes for the ice cream which can be made during the cooking of the crema

Please note that this dessert must be cooked and chilled prior to serving so leave sufficient time for this and the ice cream must be left in the freezer for a minimum of 12 hours prior to serving so best made one day in advance

—⁓—

750ml cream

250ml whole milk

150g sugar

15 egg yolks

2 sticks of cinnamon

Peel of one lemon (only the yellow part)

Place the milk and cream in a pan, then break the cinnamon sticks and add these to the pan with the lemon peel. Bring to the boil.

Mix the egg yolks with an electric whisk if possible then pour the hot milk mixture over the yolks. Add the sugar and mix well, then pour the liquid through a sieve before pouring into four mini flan or mousse dishes.

Take a deep roasting tin and place the dishes into the tin. Pour water three quarter of the way up the dishes then place into the oven for 45 minutes at 85ºC Once cooked leave to cool then refrigerate until ready to eat.

Before serving sprinkle with sugar and toast with a blowtorch, then serve with cinnamon ice cream.

CINNAMON ICE CREAM

As far as ice creams go, this really is not bad. Granted it remains high in fat and calories due to the cream and sugar content but the egg yolks, lemon peel and cinnamon bring a range of health benefits from eliminating toxins from the body, promoting a healthy nervous system. A treat star rated dish but no need to feel too guilty.

750ml whole milk

250ml fresh cream

12 egg yolks

250g sugar

2 sticks of cinnamon

1 lemon peel

A splash of cinnamon flavoured liqueur

Place the milk in a pan with the cinnamon sticks broken into two or three pieces and the lemon peel. Bring to the boil. Meanwhile, mix the egg yolks and the sugar then add the hot milk to this mixture. Return the combined mixture to the pan and bring back to the boil keeping the mixture at around 80°C. Stir until thick and smooth – it should be pourable but but thick in consistency and not runny Once the desired consistency is achieved, add the fresh cream and stir well.

Allow to cool, then place in the fridge for a minimum of 12 hours.

Once it has been left for the required time, pour through a strainer and then add the splash of liqueur. Place in an ice cream machine, then keep in the freezer until ready to use.

CASA MONTAÑA

Casa Montaña , Carrer De Josep Benlliure, 69, 46011, Valencia

On walking into this deceptive gem hidden in the heart of what was once the area that was home to the fishermen and sailors, I was immersed in the deep smell of the large wooden barrels that form the backdrop of this truly authentic tapas restaurant. Transformed from a corner shop into what is now a highly acclaimed family run restaurant, Casa Montaña has been serving simple traditional tapas to the locals, tourists and gastronomists on a daily basis , since 1994, using the finest fresh ingredients that are delivered daily. Now with a staff of 27, ten of which are chefs, and run by Emiliano Garcia Dohene and his son Alejandro Garcia Llinares, their menus are available in seven languages proving just how far many of their diners travel to experience what can only be described as truly wonderful authentic home cooked food.

Favourite dishes remain marinated tuna, sardines, tomatoes, anchovies, steak and all food is served tapas style and with the intention of it being shared between family and friends.

HABAS ESTOFADAS
STEWED BEANS

Broad beans are rich in both protein and fibre as well as providing a range of vitamins and minerals. They are an excellent source of iron thus preventing anaemia and boosting brain health and their vitamin C content boosts immunity and the production of collagen in the body. Chilli peppers are loaded with vitamin C, contain capsaicin, which is a potent anti-inflammatory, are a thermogenic and so increase the metabolism and boost heart health. This is a three star health rated dish.

INGREDIENTS FOR TEN PEOPLE
Cooking 1 hour
Please note that the beans must
be soaked in water overnight
prior to cooking

~~~

500g dried broad beans soaked
overnight in water

1 large ham bone

100g cured smoked meat of choice

150g chorizo

2 chilli peppers

10g bay leaves

10g dried mint

1 tablespoon of spicy paprika
heated in 8 tablespoons of olive
oil

Salt to season

Put all of the ingredients into a pressure cooker with enough water to cover all. Cook on a medium heat for one hour, taste and season with salt if required.

Serve a ladle of beans into a small bowl, cover with a little of the delicious spicy liquid and it is ready to go.

SARDINES

Sardines are one of the highest sources of omega 3 fatty acids on the planet which reduce inflammation in the body, raise mood and prevent depression and lower cholesterol levels. They are an excellent source of protein and bursting with vitamin B12 which promotes a healthy nervous system, boosts brain health and energy levels. They are rich in selenium, a powerful antioxidant that protects the body from illness and premature ageing as well as being a fantastic source of calcium and vitamin D. This dish is quick and simple yet incredibly nutritious. Three stars!

INGREDIENTS PER PERSON
Cooking 6-8 minutes

6 sardines
Salt
Olive oil
Lemon (to serve)

Heat a hot plate or frying pan and make a bed of salt on it – not too thick, just a decent scattering.

Place the sardines on top, drizzle with olive oil and cook for a few minutes.

Once the eyes of the sardines turn white they are ready to turn over which depending on the size of the sardines usually takes around 3 minutes.

Cook for a further 3 minutes until the sardines are cooked through and crispy and a little golden.
Place onto a plate and serve with a wedge of lemon.

SOLOMILLIO
SIMPLY STEAK

Beef is a wonderful source of protein and amino acids as well as glutathione, a wonderful antioxidant that boosts the immune system, protects against illness and disease and prevents premature ageing. Garlic has been proven to reverse early heart disease by removing the build-up of plaque in the arteries, it has anti-cancer properties and has been shown to control blood pressure levels. Garlic has the ability to balance blood sugar levels and so is beneficial for diabetics and its allicin content makes it a fabulous tonic for treating colds and infections. Olive oil promotes heart and brain health, boosts mood, has anti-cancer properties and slows down the ageing process. This dish is a powerhouse of nutrients and most definitely a three star rated dish.

INGREDIENTS PER PERSON
Cooking 8 minutes

———

200g fillet steak

1 cherry tomato

1 garlic scape chopped finely (this is the stalk of the garlic bulb readily available here in Spain but less so in England. If you are unable to locate this, then substitute with a small spring onion chopped finely and a minced clove of garlic)

Olive oil

Heat a pan to hot then place the steak into it. At the same time, place the olive oil, garlic scape and tomato into a small pan and heat until boiling then simmer while the steak cooks.

After a couple of minutes turn the steak to cook the other side. Once that side has cooked, slice the steak into cm thick slices and sear all edges.

Slice into inch size pieces then place into the centre of a plate. Place the cherry tomato on top of the steak then spoon over some of the garlic and olive oil. Season with a little salt.

HOMEMADE VALENCIAN ORANGE DESSERT

I am afraid that the oranges in this dish do not grant it a three star health rating as it is also high in calories, sugar and fat. Most definitely a TREAT rating.

INGREDIENTS FOR TWENTY PORTIONS

Cooking 20 minutes plus time to make and set the jelly.

Please note that the mascarpone mixture must be make in advance and left overnight to chill and set

—∿∿—

1.5kg mascarpone

3ltr cream

700g sugar

500g (around 27) egg yolks

11 sheets of gelatine

The grated zest of 8 oranges

Place the mascarpone, cream, sugar and zest into a pan and bring to the boil. Once it reaches boiling point, remove from the heat and add the beaten egg yolks before finally adding the gelatine. Strain through a sieve and place into a bowl. Stir well then leave for at least 24 hours in the fridge.

For the base you may use orange jelly pre-set in the base of the glass with a rich tea type biscuit added to the jelly to provide texture.

Place the creamy mixture over the top of the set jelly. Decorate with three segments of mandarins, a sprinkle of orange zest and a mint leaf.

PETIT BISTRO

Petit Bistro, Avinguda Corts Valencianes, 15, 46111, Rocafort, Valencia

Petit Bistro is a chain of restaurants in Valencia with a wonderful menu to cater for everyone but staying true to traditional Spanish foods. Young in terms of restaurants in Spain, having only being launched four years ago but already their success has seen the brand grow immensely and it is most certainly a popular place to eat. Chef Diego Oliver Gomez took the time out of his extremely busy schedule to teach me some of Petit Bistro's most popular dishes which have since become some of the most popular dishes in our home too. Delicious yet simple.

ENSALADA PETIT

Salad leaves are rich in fibre and bursting with antioxidants so protecting against illness and disease and promoting a healthy intestine and preventing constipation. Raisins are also an excellent course of fibre, full of calcium and so promote strong and healthy bones as well as balancing blood pressure and their iron content helps to prevent anaemia too. Goats cheese contains less fat and calories than other cheeses yet contains more vitamins than cows milk cheese particularly vitamins D and K making it a super bone building cheese. It is also a great source of B vitamins so promoting a healthy nervous system and boosting memory and concentration. A three star rated dish.

INGREDIENTS AT CHOICE
DEPENDING ON NUMBER OF
SERVINGS
Preparation 5 mintues

Mixed salad leaves
Raisins
Corn flakes
Goat's cheese
Honey and mustard dressing
Radishes

The quantities of ingredients here can be selected as per personal preference as there is no right or wrong.

In a large bowl place the salad leaves, raisins, cornflakes and some of the goats cheese crumbled.

Add a little olive oil and mix well.

On a large plate, drizzle some of the honey and mustard dressing before placing the salad mixture on top.

Sprinkle over a few more corn flakes, top with the rest of the goat's cheese, decorate with the sliced radish, then drizzle the honey and mustard dressing over the top.

SARTEN DE HUEVOS

There are many wonderful nutrients included in this dish from the protein and vitamin D rich eggs, to the heart healthy and mood boosting olive oil and foie is bursting with copper and iron as well as vitamin B12 which boosts memory, concentration and energy. However, foie is also high in fat and cholesterol and the method of cooking this dish is also calorific making this a one star health rated dish.

INGREDIENTS PER PERSON
Cooking 45 minutes

—⁓—

2 potatoes, peeled and sliced

2 eggs

4 or 5 large slices of
jamon Iberico

Olive oil

Black salt

2 pieces of foie gras

Salt

Black pepper

Place the potatoes on a roasting tray with some olive oil and salt and pepper and roast for around 25-30 minutes at 200ºC. Remove from the oven. In a large frying pan, add a couple of table spoons of olive oil and heat on high before adding the roasted potatoes. Stir and slightly press the potatoes to mash them slightly.

At the same time, add a little olive oil to another pan and sauté the foie for four to five minutes on each side until golden.

In a third pan, add a little oil to a pan and crack the two eggs whole into the pan and fry until cooked through for a couple of minutes.

To plate up, ideally use mini pans like we have in this photo but any dish of a similar size will suffice.

First add the potatoes to the bottom of the pan, then place the jamon around the side, place the eggs on top, then finish with the foie.
Season with the black salt.

SALMON WITH SPINACH AND VEGETABLES AND A DILL SAUCE

Salmon is rich in omega 3 fatty acids which aid healthy joints and skin and boosts heart and brain health. Spinach is rich in calcium, magnesium, iron and zinc as well as vitamins A, B6 and K. It is a wonderful bone building food, fantastic for eye health, muscles, blood pressure, boosts the metabolism and even speeds up wound healing. Serving with vegetables of your choice simply increases the fibre and vitamin and mineral content of this already wonderful dish. A three star health rating.

INGREDIENTS DEPENDENT ON NUMBER OF SERVINGS

The dill sauce will be sufficient for 12-18 servings and can be stored in the fridge for up to three days.

Cooking 10-15 minutes depending on preference for the cook of the salmon

---

Dill sauce

600g cream

300g fish stock

20g butter

10g lemon juice

Black pepper

25g fresh dill

10g diced onion

One salmon fillet per person

Olive oil

Butter

Spinach

For the dill sauce: Place all the ingredients into a blender and blend until smooth. Refrigerate, then heat when required.

You will note that I have not written quantities here for the above ingredients as it will be dependent on the number of people being served and preference. Despite looking fabulous, this is an incredibly simple dish to make.

Steam vegetables of your choice (we used asparagus, carrots, broccoli, cauliflower and courgette).

Whilst the vegetables are steaming, melt a little butter in a pan and place the salmon fillets skin side down and cook on a fairly high heat to crisp the skin.

Heat a little olive oil in a pan and add a handful of spinach per person. Cook until wilted down then turn off the heat and leave to crisp a little.

Once the skin is crispy, turn the salmon fillets to brown the top of the fish.

To plate up – it works really well if you use a ring to place the vegetables into so that they are of a

Steamed vegetables

Dill sauce

Olive oil

uniform shape on the plate and it looks really neat. Place the ring on the plate, fill with the vegetables then carefully remove it.

On one side of the vegetables place the crisped spinach and then carefully place the salmon fillet on the other side.

Top with some of the dill sauce that has been heated and a sprig of fresh dill to finish it off.

VANILLA CHEESECAKE WITH FRESH BERRIES

This is simply a divine dessert which looks and tastes wonderful, but it is a TREAT rating.

INGREDIENTS FOR
TEN-TWELVE PEOPLE
Cooking 1 hours 15 minutes plus
cooling and chilling time

—〜〜—

150g digestive biscuits
75g butter
900g full fat cream cheese
200g caster sugar
200ml sour cream
3 tablespoons of plain flour
3 eggs plus one egg yolk beaten slightly
2 teaspoons of vanilla extract
Fresh berries for decorating

Preheat the oven to 180ºC and then grease and line the base of a cake tin with detachable sides – 9 inch would be ideal.

Place the digestives in a plastic bag and crush with a rolling pin until they are fine crumbs. Melt the butter in a pan and add the bread crumbs. Stir until combined before pouring into the cake tin and pressing down in an even layer.

Place into the oven and bake for around ten minutes until golden. Remove and set aside. Reduce the oven temperature to 160ºC.

In a large bowl beat together the cream cheese and sugar until smooth then add the sour cream and flour and beat again. Gradually add the beaten eggs and vanilla essence mixing well before adding more. Be careful not to whisk as this will add in too much air which will affect the smooth surface of the cheesecake.

Once all the eggs and vanilla essence have been added and combined, pour this mixture onto the cooled biscuit base. Place in the oven and bake for 45 minutes.

It is ready once the surface is set but the cream cheese still wobbles.

Turn off the oven, open the door and leave the cheesecake to cool in the open oven to prevent the cracking of the surface.

Once cool, remove from the oven and remove from the tin. Decorate with fresh berries and serve.

FOOD AND FUN

Food and Fun, Carrer De La Llanterna, 6, 46001, Valencia

Food and Fun is a wonderful rustic open plan kitchen/cooking school right in the heart of the city of Valencia. Opened in 2009 by Felicidad Juan whose travels all over the world ignited her passion to learn more about the foods she was eating and how to create them and this process led her to realise that she was among many who would love the opportunity to do the same. After the birth of her children Felicidad was forced to leave her job and spent her spare time recreating the meals she had learnt on her travels for family and friends – all of whom advised her that she should open a restaurant. With no qualifications in cooking and no interest in being a restaurant owner in the then difficult recession of Spain, one day wandering through the city she came across the empty premises that would soon fulfil her dreams.

She sought the advice of her friends who were architects, bartered with the owner to achieve a rent that she could afford and shortly after Food and Fun was born. Bringing together people from all walks of life, all nationalities for not only an education in cooking but also a social event ranging from breakfast meetings to whole days learning to cook elaborate three course meals. We definitely had fun cooking some extremely popular traditional Spanish meals with Felicidad and her Food and Fun team.

SALMOREJO CORDOBES

Tomatoes are rich in beta carotene and the antioxidant lycopene, the combination of which provide a powerful boost to heart health and may lower cholesterol. Lycopene also aids strong and healthy bones. Wonderful for promoting healthy eyes and skin as well as giving the immune system a boost. Couple all these wonderful qualities with the heart healthy olive oil and the immune boosting garlic and this really is a nutrient rich dish. A three star health rated dish. This is a type of cold soup similar to gazpacho but much denser and more flavourful.

INGREDIENTS FOR
FOUR PEOPLE
Cooking 15 minutes plus time in
advance to cook and cool the
eggs

———

1kg ripe tomatoes
100g homemade thick bread
crumbs
1 garlic clove
100g cooked chopped
pancetta/bacon or jamon iberico
3 hardboiled eggs cooled and
peeled
Salt
150g olive oil

Wash the tomatoes and cut each into quarters. Place into a blender and blend until smooth.

Add the bread and leave for five minutes to soak.

Add the clove of garlic then blend again. While blending slowly, add the olive oil to the mixture – this process will take approximately one to two minutes.

Pour into bowls.

Grate the boiled eggs and on one side of the bowl place a layer of the egg followed by a layer of the bacon next to it, not on top.

Drizzle with olive oil and serve.

HAM AND MUSHROOM CROQUETES

Mushrooms are low in carbohydrates and calories yet rich in fibre, B vitamins and protein. They are a natural and powerful anti-inflammatory food and boost the immune system. Onion is also a wonderful immune boosting food and also aids the detoxification of the body. They an anti-cancer food, rich in vitamin C and so boost the production of collagen in the body required for healthy muscles, skin, joints and ligaments. However, this dish is fried and contains significant amounts of fat and calories and so is a one star health rated dish.

INGREDIENTS FOR FOUR PEOPLE

Cooking 30 minutes

Please note the first part of this recipe requires cooking in advance and storing in the fridge overnight

——

150g plain flour

100ml olive oil

One onion

200g mushrooms

150g ham

1 ltr milk

Salt

Pepper

1 teaspoon of nutmeg

2 eggs, beaten

Fine breadcrumbs

Chop the ham and mushrooms and sauté with the olive oil. Add the onion and the flour and stir continuously for three minutes. Heat the milk in a separate pan and slowly add to the mixture stirring continually and heat until the desired consistency is achieved which is quite thick.

Remove from the heat and allow to cool before storing in the fridge overnight.

Place some plain flour in a bowl. In a separate bowl, place some beaten eggs. Take small handfuls of the chilled mixture and roll into balls. First, dip into the egg mixture and cover fully, then roll into the flour and finally roll in and coat completely with the breadcrumbs.

Repeat this until you have used all the chilled mixture.

Heat enough sunflower oil in a pan until hot to cover the croquetes, then place into the oil. Cook for a couple of minutes on each side until golden. Remove from the oil and place onto some kitchen paper to soak up any excess oil then plate up and enjoy!

CALAMARES A LA ROMANA

Calamari itself is actually low in calories, high in protein and contains no carbohydrates. It is an excellent source of B vitamin so aiding a healthy nervous system, brain function and boosting energy. Containing selenium and vitamin E also makes it a wonderful fertility boosting food. However, this particular recipe involves frying the calamari hence its health star rating drops to one star.

INGREDIENTS FOR
FOUR PEOPLE
Cooking 5 minutes not including
the cleaning of the calamari

—◊—

400g calamari
3 eggs
200g flour
Oil for frying

Clean the calamari, removing the guts, eyes and mouth, then cut into slices of 1cm. Add a little salt.

Place the flour in one bowl and the beaten eggs in another bowl.

Firstly, dip the calamari into the eggs then coat fully in the flour.

Fry for literally a couple of minutes in very hot oil. Remove and place onto kitchen paper before plating up, adding a little more rock salt and grating over a little lemon zest.

Delicious served with a lemon mayo dip.

TORTITAS DE CAMARON

Prawns are a low fat source of protein also containing potassium, calcium and vitamins E and A. They contain no carbohydrates and are a source of those wonderful omega 3 fatty acids that boost heart and brain health and reduce inflammation in the body. Containing selenium and zinc, they boost skin health, fertility and the immune system. They also promote strong and healthy bones. Chickpea flour contains more fibre and protein than regular flour and is gluten free too. It contains a perfect ratio of calcium and magnesium so promoting bone health. It is known to balance blood sugar levels and balance the PH level in the body. This is a three star health rated dish, so enjoy guilt free.

INGREDIENTS FOR
FOUR PEOPLE
Cooking 10 minutes

—∿∿—

75g wheat flour
75g chickpea flour
300g water
Half a chopped onion
100g camarones (tiny baby prawns)
Chopped parsley

Mix all the ingredients in a bowl until a smooth light paste in achieved.

In a frying pan heat a little olive oil. Using a ladle, ladle one portion into the pan (like making pancakes) and cook for a few minutes on each side until golden. Repeat until all the mixture has been used. Plate and decorate with the chopped parsley.

FLAMENQUINES

Chicken is a great source of protein and also contains calcium, potassium, iron and magnesium resulting in it protecting against anaemia, boosting bone health and the immune system too. It is also fantastic for eye health due to its retinol, lycopene and beta carotene content. Its vitamin B content promotes a healthy nervous system and it has also been shown to regulate cortisol, the stress hormone. However, in this recipe the chicken is fried and so this is a one star health rated dish.

INGREDIENTS FOR
FOUR PEOPLE
Cooking 20 minutes
Please take care when handling raw chicken. Wash hands thoroughly and ensure separate boards, plates and utensils are used for the raw chicken and washed well after use.

—⁓—

4 chicken fillets
4 long slices of jamon Serrano
100g flour
2 large eggs
200g fine bread crumbs
Salt and pepper to season

Wrap the chicken fillets in cling film and using a rolling pin, beat until flattened.

Season with salt and pepper then add a slice of ham to each flattened chicken breast.

Roll each fillet and secure at each end with wooded toothpicks.

Dip each rolled fillet into the flour, then into the beaten egg mixture and finally coat in the breadcrumbs.

Heat enough oil in a pan to cover the rolled fillets until hot, add the fillets and cook for around 6-8 minutes until golden brown and cooked through.

Remove from the oil, place onto kitchen paper to remove any excess oil, slice in half and serve.

CHIPIRONES EN SU TINTA

This translates as squid in their dye. Quite possibly not the most attractive looking dish but delicious and super popular here in Spain. We rarely see dishes of this type in the UK but we could be missing out. Squid ink is actually rich in antioxidants so protecting the body from all those damaging free radicals that lead to illness and disease and preventing anti-ageing. Naturally rich in dopamine and so increasing concentration, memory and mental focus. It provides a healthy amount of iron, boosting red blood cells and studies have shown it to boost the cancer killer cells. The squid itself is both low in carbohydrates and fat and actually lowers cholesterol levels. It is rich in vitamin B2 which has been shown to prevent migraines as well as boosting energy levels. A great source of protein, naturally anti-bacterial and anti-inflammatory it may reduce the symptoms of arthritis and asthma. Impress your guests and boost their health at the same time with this three star health rated meal.

INGREDIENTS FOR
FOUR PEOPLE
Cooking 35 minutes

—ww—

5 onions
4 small sachets of calamari tinta
(dye)
50g squid
10g dark bitter chocolate
Olive oil
1 clove of garlic
3 green peppers
400ml of white wine

Chop the pepper and the onions and fry until soft. Add the chopped garlic, then the wine and leave to cook until the alcohol has evaporated.

Add the sachets of dye, leave to cook for a few minutes and watch the mixture turn to a deep black colour. Remove from the heat and blend.

Add the blended mixture back to the pan then add the chocolate and the squid, cleaned and with the spines and mouths removed.

Cook for approximately 15 minutes until the squid have expanded and cooked through.

POLLO AL VINO

Chicken is a great source of protein and also contains calcium, potassium, iron and magnesium resulting in it protecting against anaemia, boosting bone health and the immune system too. It is also fantastic for eye health due to its retinol, lycopene and beta carotene content. Its vitamin B content promotes a healthy nervous system and it has also been shown to regulate cortisol, the stress hormone. The garlic boosts the immune system, protects against colds and infections, boosts heart health and the olive oil boosts both heart and brain health, reduces inflammation in the body and can kill harmful bacteria. This is a two star health rated dish.

INGREDIENTS FOR
FOUR PEOPLE
Cooking 40 minutes
Please take care when handling raw chicken. Wash hands thoroughly and ensure separate boards, plates and utensils are used for the raw chicken and washed well after use.

1 whole chicken cut into legs, breasts and thighs
1 whole head of garlic
2ltr of white wine
Salt and pepper to season
Olive oil
1 bay leaf

Heat the olive oil in a large pan and add the chicken pieces, season and brown on all sides. Slice the whole garlic in half and add to the pan before adding all the white wine.

Cook for around 30 minutes until the chicken is cooked through, the alcohol has evaporated and reduced and the liquid thickened.
Plate up and enjoy.

ENSALADA RUSA

This is a wonderfully tasty yet nutritious dish that can be served as a side dish or with salad as a main course. The carrots provide heaps of beta carotene boosting both eye and heart health and the eggs are a wonderful source of vitamin D and choline which is a vital macronutrient required for physiological functions such as metabolism, nerve control and muscle functioning. Eggs also provide selenium which is a powerful anti-inflammatory. Potatoes contain a resistant starch which has been shown to control blood sugar levels and boost digestive heath and they provide a wonderful boost of antioxidants so protecting the body from illness and disease. Tuna is a fantastic protein source and rich in omega 3 fatty acids resulting in a healthier heart and brain! The mayonnaise does add fat and calories but the amount to be added is personal choice so no need to overdo it. A three star health rated dish (as long as the mayonnaise added is not a huge amount).

INGREDIENTS FOR FOUR PEOPLE

Cooking 30 minutes plus cooling time prior to assembling and serving

—✳—

1kg potatoes

400g carrots

5 large eggs

Mayonnaise

Salt

2 large cooked tuna steaks or 2 large tins of tuna (depending on preference)

200g green beans

Peel and chop the potatoes and carrots.

In a pan of boiling water cook the potatoes for around 10 minutes then add the chopped carrots and whole green beans and cook for a further 8 minutes until cooked. Remove and allow to cool.

Hard boil the eggs and leave to cool (around ten minutes in the pan with boiling water).

Chop the shelled hard boiled eggs and place in a large bowl. Add the cooled potatoes and vegetables then add the tuna. Add mayonnaise – the amount to your desire but ensure all ingredients are coated.

Serve and enjoy.
This works really well served in large lettuce leaves.

ARROZ CON LECHE

This dish does have some added sugar but despite this, it also provides a wonderful range of vitamins and minerals. The milk provides calcium and some protein as well as B vitamins, calcium and magnesium making it an all round bone building food. Cinnamon protects the heart, reduces inflammation in the body, lowers blood sugar levels and protects against viruses and infections. It is a carbohydrate and therefore a wonderful source of energy for the body. It is also rich in calcium and iron, niacin and vitamin D as well as antioxidants. It is also naturally gluten free. Lemon peel actually contains 5-10 times more vitamins than the juice itself. It eradicates toxins from the body, is rich in both calcium and vitamin C boosting bone health and has been shown to lower cholesterol. A two star health rated dish.

INGREDIENTS FOR
FOUR PEOPLE
Cooking one hour
Please note that this dessert requires time to cool and chill prior to serving

—∾∾—

1.5ltr whole milk
115g pudding or uncooked white rice
100g sugar
2 slices of lemon peel
2 slices of orange peel
1 cinnamon stick
1 teaspoon of vanilla essence
Ground cinnamon to decorate

In a large pan place the milk, the lemon and orange peel, the vanilla essence and the cinnamon stick. Bring to the boil.

Once boiling, add the sugar and the rice and stir well.

Cook for around 40-45 minutes, stirring every five minutes until the rice is soft.

Remove from the pan, place in a bowl and chill,

Once chilled remove the cinnamon stick and the peel, then serve into bowls.

Dust with the ground cinnamon and devour.

FEDERAL CAFÉ

Carrer de l'Ambaixador Vich, 15, 46002 València

Breakfast in Spain really is not the same experience that most UK households will have on a daily basis. The Spanish never eat in a hurry. There are very few if any 'food to go' places in Valencia city and I have never seen anyone walking down a street eating a sandwich. The Spanish sit down, savour and enjoy every single meal and breakfast is no different. I cannot imagine anyone in Spain eating a bowl of cereal whilst dressing or drying their hair in a bid to get out of the door to work or school on time. In fact, the Spanish tend to eat very little on first waking but eat their main 'breakfast' or almuerzo which we would refer to as brunch at their mid-morning break which they take time to sit down and enjoy. When you try out some of these recipes, you will understand why they wish to take their time and enjoy these wonderful breakfast foods.

I was thrilled that the wonderful Federal Café in Valencia city was prepared to open its doors, collaborate with me in this book and share with both me and you some of its wonderful recipes and delicious traditional Spanish breakfast foods.

Federal café not only serves breakfasts but is open all day serving fabulous lunches and dinners too but it is famous for both its wonderful breakfasts and desserts. Originating as far back as 1905 and working out of a listed building in the heart of the city, maintaining the original features both internally and externally with huge tall ceilings and magnificent natural light permeating the restaurant from every angle from the multitude of tall windows. It is most definitely a place of both peace and harmony that oozes relaxation.

Diana Resurreccion Arcas is the director whilst Antoinete Hung from Venezuela is responsible for the wonderful breads, cakes and all things deliciously sweet. Antoinette has been working as a chef from the age of 18 but did not move to Spain until 2012 when she went to Barcelona to study pasteleria, In July she took the helm at Federal Café.

BUÑELOS DE CALABAZA PUMPKIN DOUGHNUTS

As far as doughnuts go, these really are pretty impressive. Pumpkin is rich in fibre, aiding digestion and keeping you feeling fuller for longer. Bursting with beta carotene and vitamin C boosting both eye health and the immune system and aiding the production of collagen required for healthy skin, bones and ligaments. Eggs provide added protein as well as vitamin D and those heart healthy omega 3 fatty acids. They are fried in oil which does result in a one star health rating.

INGREDIENTS FOR EIGHT PORTIONS
Cooking 1 hour

125g flour
300g pumpkin
3g yeast
2 eggs
25g sugar
Zest of one lemon
Half a teaspoon of salt

Peel the pumpkin, remove the seeds and chop into chunks before placing in a pan with water and bringing to the boil. Simmer until the pumpkin is soft, then drain and blend to make a creamy puree. Reserve the water for later.

Separate the egg yolks from the egg whites. Whisk the egg whites until stiff and forming peaks and set aside.

Sieve the flour into a bowl and add the yeast, the sugar, the salt, the orange zest and the egg yolks and mix until it forms a dough. Add 12 tablespoons of the pumpkin water, then add the pumpkin puree and mix well.

Fold in half of the egg whites gently followed by the other half once fully incorporated.

Place the mixture into a piping bag.

In a small pan, place enough oil to cover the size of the doughnuts and heat until hot. Squeeze portion sizes of the mixture into the hot oil using a knife to cut off the dough when enough mixture has been piped. Cook until golden on both sides before draining on kitchen paper. Sprinkle with sugar or cinnamon and serve.

CHURROS

Churros definitely look and taste amazing, however nutritionally they simply have a TREAT rating.

INGREDIENTS FOR TWELVE
PORTIONS
Cooking 25 minutes

—₩—

250ml water
120g flour
One pinch of salt
20g butter
Sunflower oil
200g sugar

Heat the water in a pan then add the butter and salt. Once the water is boiling add the flour and continue to stir with a wooden spoon until a dough forms. If the dough is really hard then add a little extra water.

Remove from the pan and wrap in cling film, then leave until it is luke warm.

Place the lukewarm dough into a piping bag with a notched edge.

Heat the oil in a pan until hot before piping in long strips of the dough.

Cook on both sides until golden, then remove and drain on kitchen paper. Sprinkle with sugar or icing sugar. Best served with a cup of melted chocolate or thick hot chocolate.

MADALENAS

Well, who would not want to eat cake for breakfast? Delicious undoubtedly but with a TREAT rating so maybe not an everyday choice.

INGREDIENTS FOR TWELVE
PORTIONS
Cooking 30 minutes

———

250g brown sugar
5 eggs
250ml sunflower oil
250g flour
15g yeast
10g salt
Zest of one lemon
Zest of one orange
3 tablespoons of brown sugar for decoration

Pre heat the oven to 165°C.

In a bowl mix the eggs with the sugar. Once mixed add the flour and the yeast as well as the salt and orange and lemon zests.

Finally add the oil and beat until fully incorporated.

Place muffin cases into a muffin tray and fill until just over halfway with the mixture.

Sprinkle with the brown sugar and place into the oven for around 20 minutes.

To check if fully cooked, place a skewer into the centre of one of the cakes and if it comes out clean, they are ready to remove from the oven.

GALLETAS MARIA

I am afraid that these delicious cookies have a TREAT rating. These delicious biscuits are a staple breakfast food in Spain and are used in so many other recipes as well.

INGREDIENTS FOR TWENTY
PORTIONS
Cooking 35 minutes
Please note that the dough needs to be left in the fridge for two hours prior to rolling, cutting and baking so allow sufficient time for this

———

300g flour
2 egg yolks
150g butter
40g icing sugar
20ml water
Cookie cutter

Mix the butter and sugar and once combined add the egg yolks one by one and then the water.

Once mixed well, add the flour.

Place the dough into the fridge for two hours. Pre heat the oven to 165°C.

Roll out the dough and using the cookie cutter, cut as many cookies as possible, re-rolling the leftover dough if required.

Place the cookies onto a baking sheet lined with baking paper and place in the oven for around 10/12 minutes until the edges of the cookies start to turn golden.

COCKTAILS
IVAN & HECTOR TALENS

A book on Spanish gastronomy just would not be complete without some wonderful cocktails and I have been lucky enough to collaborate with two 'celebrities' in the world of cocktail making in Spain – brothers Ivan and Hector Talens.

Ivan started by saying he is enamoured by cocteleria which he sees as both art and passion. Both brothers boast years of experience in hotels and restaurants and have won an array of awards due to their cocktail making skills. In 2012, Ivan opened his first cocktail bar, Cocktail Clam, which went on to win the Coaster award in 2015. He then went on to open Magatzem which is a store specializing in cocteleria, wine and spirits. He is currently the president of the ABCV in Valencia which is the association of barmen. Hector launched Mes que Barmans in 2010 which is a catering cocktail barman service alongside his brother and his mentor, Ivan. The cocktails that they have shared with us are sophisticated, sexy and delicious. Now you can impress your guests with your cocktail making skills too!

ROCAFULL

This is a mysterious cocktail that originates from Valencia. It is actually named after Doctor Rocafull who went regularly to a cafeteria in Valencia and always ordered an iced coffee with brandy and egg white. The drink became extremely popular and so they named it after the doctor who first drank it. Prepare this drink in a cocktail shaker with ice.

INGREDIENTS PER SERVING

4cl of brandy
15cl of frozen coffee (like slush)
2cl liquid sugar
2cl egg white
Shake vigorously then serve in a tall glass and top with grated lime zest.

AGUA DE VALENCIA

Agua de Valencia is a cocktail that originated in Valencia with a base of Cava or Champagne, orange juice, vodka and gin. It was developed primarily in 1959 for Constante Gil in La Cerveceria De Madrid de Valencia. For a whole decade it was only known by a small group of clients and it was not until 1970 when it became a well-known evening drink in the bars of Valencia. Since then it has become hugely popular.

INGREDIENTS PER SERVING
2cl vodka
2cl gin
15cl orange juice
Sugar (optional)

~~~

Prepare directly in a tall glass

Add ice, then fill to the top with
Cava or Champagne

LA MAMADETA

This is a typical drink of the fiestas of Santa Tecla which began in 1321 when the relic of the arm of Saint Tecla arrived in the city of Tarragona, having come from Armenia. Nowadays nobody would understand the fiesta of Santa Tecla without the popular drink known as La Mamadeta and its main ingredient, Chartreuse, which is a French liqueur. This liqueur has had links with Tarragona for centuries, the origin of which is thought to be mysterious and magical.

INGREDIENTS PER SERVING
4cl Chartreuse
14cl lemon granizado (iced
lemon slush)

—◆—

Prepare in a cocktail shaker

Shake vigorously and serve in a
tall glass

MOJITO ESPAÑOL

Since 2006 the wine company 'Torres' have worked to create a Spanish cocktail which combines the classics – the mojito and Brandy Torres 15. They have retrieved the concept and furthermore they have substituted the classic rum and the soda in this version is ginger ale.

INGREDIENTS PER SERVING
4cl Brandy Torres 15

1 bunch of fresh mint

2 quarters of lemon

16g brown sugar

4cl ginger ale

A sprig of fresh mint to decorate

Pull the mint leaves off the branch and place in a glass with the sliced lime quarters and the sugar. Add ice to fill ¾ of the glass then add the brandy. Fill the glass to the top with the ginger ale, then stir. Top with the sprig of mint and add a straw.

SANGRIA

This wonderful famous Spanish cocktail needs no introduction!

INGREDIENTS PER SERVING

4cl Brandy Torres 15

16cl red wine

2cl sugar syrup

1 cinnamon stick

Slices of orange and lemon

Lemon juice

———⁂———

Prepare directly in a large round glass.

NAVARRO BODEGUERO

100 Cardenal Benlloch, Valencia 46021

O n arriving in Spain, I very quickly came to realise that wine plays a huge part in the culture here and is a vital part of almost every meal. It isn't drinking to excess but rather complementing the flavours of the food with contrasting tones of the wines specially selected for each dish. Each mouthful is savoured and enjoyed.

Being teetotal all of my life, I literally had no idea about wines whatsoever but felt that it was important to include them in this book given their importance to Spanish Gastronomy. I arranged to visit a very well-known winery in the city to introduce me to the world of wines and educate me on why they are so important – and this visit actually turned out to be an amazing day and incredibly interesting.

Navarro Bodeguero is a family-run winery and currently run by the fourth generation of this family yet it is clear to see that the passion for wines burns as intensely in this generation as it did in that of their great grandfather. I was lucky enough to receive my lesson in wines from the current owner and manager, David Navarro.

The taste and quality of wines is dependent on three things; the climate in the area of the vineyard; the type of grapes/age of vineyard; and the wood and barrel

In Spain there are three different climates which greatly affect the type and quality of wine produced: the Mediterranean climate along the East and South; the Continental climate of Central and Western Spain; and the Atlantic Northern region.

Each climate differs in temperature, humidity, rainfall and type of land and all of these factors determine the type of wine produced. Spain itself is in the top three wine producing countries in the world along with France and Italy. They have invested huge amounts of money in the process of wine making over the years and sell in bulk quantities across the world. However, the Spanish wines tend not to be viewed as prestigious or coveted as those of France and Italy but what that does mean is that you can actually purchase a bottle of high quality wine for a really reasonable price.

True wine experts know never to cup their glass in their hands. The reason for this is that our

bodies are usually around 36/37oC yet the wine will be of a lower temperature. For example, a perfect red wine will be served at 16oC, cupping it in your hand as opposed to holding the glass by the stem will raise the temperature of the wine and negatively affect the flavour.

The main types of wine are: white; red; sparkling; rose; young – bottled straight from picking; crianza – matured in the barrel for between 6 months and one year; reserva – matured for between 1-2 years; Gran Reserva – matured for a minimum of 3 years.

David explained to me that when choosing a wine to compliment a food, he looks to 'marry' the flavours. If eating a sweet food, to balance the flavour the wine should be slightly acidic. It is all about balancing. So according to my expert here are the Spanish wines you should be choosing to accompany your home made Spanish dishes:

White Fish/Mussels
Type of grapes – *Verdejo*
Brands of wines – Jose Pariente, Marques de Riscal

Prawns, Lobster, Tuna, Sardines, Anchovies
Type of grapes – *Godello*
Brands of wines – Louro, Guitian, Oluar do Sil

Seafood Paella/Cod Fishcakes
Type of grapes – *Xarel.lo*
Brands of wines – Sumarroca, Recaredo

Meats/Pork/Ham/Lamb
Type of grapes – Tempranillo of either Toro or Ribera regions
Brands of wines – Almirez, Tomas, Postigo, Aalto, Termes

Steak Tartare/Meatballs
Type of grapes – Garnacha from either Rioja or Aragon regions
Brands of wines – Peña el gato, Tres Picos, Fagus

Kidney Beans/Lentils/Bread Dishes
Sparkling wines – Recaredo, Mirgin, Gramona, Sumarroca
Brands of wines – Monastrell, Clio, Estrecho, Casa Castillo, Tarima Hill

Ensaladas/Green Caviar
Vino Rosado – Bobal
Brands of wines – Al Vent, Pasion de Bobal, Caprasia

Patatas Bravas/Tortillas
White wine – Type of grapes – Viura
Brands of wines – Vina Gravonia, Vivanco, Hacienda Lopez de Haro

Desserts

Tiramisu/Ice Cream/Cheesecake
Type of Grapes – Monastrell Dulce
Brands of wines – Mataro, Afterez, Dolc Demendoza

Fried Milk/Rice pudding/Caramel Flan/Custard Desserts
Type of Grapes – Moscatel Dulce
Brands of wines – Enrique Mendoza, Fusta Nova

Muesli and yoghurt/Almond tart/Cinnamon Cream
Type of grapes – Pedro Ximenez
Brands of wines – Noe, Donzoilo, Duquesa

So now you are fully educated on making the perfect choice of wines to complement your perfect Spanish menu!

RECIPES

Ajo-rriero (Garlic potato and cod puree) 154
Almond tart meringue 158
Almond tart 102
Apple, almond and raisin cake 232
Arnadi 138
Arroz con leche 222
Bean and pork stew 168
Beef medallions with potato discs and a rich red wine sauce 82
Beef 18, 19, 46, 70, 82, 90, 124, 190
    Steak tartare with frozen mustard ice cream 68
    Finest aged fillet of beef 46
    Rabo del Toro 124
    Solomillio 190
Bizcocho de soletilla 173
Black Pudding 18, 156, 168, 184
    Mocilla de Burgos 184
Bread with tomato and olive oil 235
Buñelos de calabaza (Pumpkin doughnuts) 226
Calamari 108, 144, 210, 216
    Calamares a la Romana 210
    Chipirones en su tinta 216
    Pan fried calamari 144
Caldereta de langoste (Lobster, clams and potatoes) 96
Caramel flan 108
Catalan Cream with Cinnamon ice cream 178
Chicken 18, 52, 168, 214, 218
    Flameniquines 214
    Pollo al vino 218
Chipirones en su tinta 216
Churros 227
Cinnamon cream with warm chocolate sauce 56
Cocido Madrileñas (Mother's Stew) 18

Cocktails:
    Agua de Valencia (Vodka, gin, orange juice) 238
    La Mamadeta (Chartreuse, lemon) 239
    Mojito Espanol (Brandy, lemon, ginger ale) 240
    Rocafull (Brandy, coffee) 236
    Sangria (Brandy, red wine) 242
    Sweet Vermouth straws 12
Cod pil pil 106
Cod profiteroles 104
Cod, fresh 104, 106, 154
    Garlic potato and cod puree 154
Cod, smoked 51, 59
    Smoked Cod Croquettes 59
Coffee cheesecake 92
Crema Catalan con helado de carela 178
Cuajada 64, 92, 128
Cuttlefish, cauliflower, garlic and smoked pancetta with rice 62
Ensalada petit 194
Ensalada Rusa 220
Ensalada Valenciana 132
Esgarrat 51
Fabada austriana (Bean and pork stew) 168
Fideau 108
Finest aged fillet of beef 46
Flameniquines 214
Foie gras with praline, black toasted sesame seeds 80
Fresh Asparagus and Caviar Salad 14

Fresh strawberry ice cream 36
Fried ice cream 74
Fried milk 120
Frozen melon and yoghurt, cucumber and basil 32
Galletas Maria biscuits 230
Garden tortilla 166
Garlic potato and cod puree 154
Gazpacho Manchego 162
Greek yoghurt with fresh and dried berries 20
Guisantes lagrima (Green caviar) 43
Habas estofadas (Stewed beans) 182
Hake barbels pil pil 45
Ham and Mushroom Croquettes 208
Kidney beans with pork 113
Lamb Tacos 24
Lamb with broad beans 164
Lamb 24, 114, 164
    Roasted baby lamb 114
Leche frita (Fried milk) 120
Leche merengada with fartons 170
Lentijas de la baneza 152
Lobster 100, 108
Lobster, clams and potatoes 96
Lubina a la sal (Salted seabass)146
Madalenas 228
Mango Tiramisu 84
Marinated tuna 118
Meatballs in a curry sauce 90
Mejilliones 186
Migas saladas (Salty breadcrumbs) 156
Mocilla de Burgos 184
Mother's Stew 18
Mushrooms 28, 162, 208
Mussels (fresh) 16, 141, 186
Mussels (tinned) 16
Mussels Escabache 16
Octopus with artichoke puree 27
Octopus with Salsa Romescu and paprika oil 134
Olla de calabaza (Pan of pumpkin) 126
Oxtail 124
Paella Valenciana 53
Pan fried calamari 144
Pan of pumpkin 126
Pan seared tuna steak with stir fried vegetables and basil aioli 72
Patatas bravas 98
Pollo al vino 218
Pork 27, 90, 113, 116, 152, 156, 168
    Bean and pork stew 168
Roasted piglet 116
Potatoes 18, 59, 82, 88, 98, 100, 104, 126, 134, 154, 166, 196, 220
    Caldereta de langoste 96
    Patatas bravas 98
    Spanish Tortilla 88
Prawns 96, 100, 108, 136, 141, 212
    Tortitas de camaron 212
Pulses:
    Broad beans (dried) 164, 182
        Habas estofadas (Stewed beans) 182
        Lamb with broad beans 164
    Butter beans (dried) 168
    Chickpeas 18

Kidney beans (dried) 113
Lima beans 53, 165
White beans, dried 126
Pumpkin 126, 138, 226
    Arnadi 138
    Buñelos de calabaza 226
Rabo de toro (Oxtail) 124
Red King Prawns 96
Rice pudding roll with apricot compote 173
Rice:
    Paella 53, 62
    Pudding 174, 222
Roasted baby lamb 114
Roasted piglet 116
Salmon with spinach & vegetables in a dill sauce 198
Salmorejo Cordobes 205
Salpicon de mariscos o frutos del mar 141
Salsa Espanola 27, 30
Salted seabass 146
Salty breadcrumbs 156
Sardines 188
Sarten de Huevos 196
Scallops 142
    Zamburiñas afeira 142
Seabass 146
    Lubina a la sal 146
Seafood casserole 136
Slow coal grilled tuna with carrot cream and salsa Perigaux 30
Smoked Cod Croquettes 59
Solomillo 190
Spanish tart 128
Spanish Tortilla 88
Splash of seafood 141
Steak tartare with frozen mustard ice cream 68
Stewed beansn 182
Strawberries and cream 148
Sweet caramel cheesecake 64
Tarta de Santiaga clasica (Santiago Cake) 176
Tomatoes 28, 53, 62, 78, 100, 132, 134, 136, 152, 162, 164, 190, 205
    Salmorejo Cordobes 205
Torrija with vanilla ice cream 48
Tortilla hortelena guisada (Garden tortilla) 166
Tortitas de camaron 212
Tuna (fresh) 30, 72, 118
    Marinated tuna 118
    Pan seared tuna steak with stir fried vegetables and basil aioli 72
    Slow coal grilled tuna with carrot cream and salsa Perigaux 30
Tuna (tinned in oil) 132, 220
Turron ice cream 38
Valencian orange dessert 192
Vanilla cheesecake with fresh berries 202
Watermelon Gazpacho 78
Whipped ice cream with eclairs 170
Wine guide 247-8
Wine: red 28, 82
Wine: white 90, 116, 164, 216, 218
Yoghurt: Greek 20, 84, 128
Yoghurt: live 32
Zamburiñas afeira 142